GRAPHIC LIBRARY™

STEM ADVENTURES

THE AMAZING STORY OF
SPACE TRAVEL

MAX AXIOM
STEM ADVENTURES

by Agnieszka Biskup

illustrated by Pop Art Properties

Consultant:
Jeffrey A. Hoffman, PhD
Former NASA Astronaut
Professor of the Practice of Aerospace Engineering
Massachusetts Institute of Technology (MIT)
Cambridge, Massachusetts

CAPSTONE PRESS
a capstone imprint

Graphic Library is published by Capstone Press,
1710 Roe Crest Drive, North Mankato, Minnesota 56003
www.capstonepub.com

Library of Congress Cataloging-in-Publication Data
Biskup, Agnieszka.
The amazing story of space travel : Max Axiom STEM adventures / by Agnieszka Biskup ; illustrated by Pop Art Properties.
pages cm.—(Graphic library. STEM adventures.)
Summary: "In graphic novel format, follows Max Axiom as he explains how astronauts travel to and from outer space"—Provided by publisher.
Audience: Grade 4 to 6.
Includes bibliographical references and index.
ISBN 978-1-4765-0124-6 (library binding)
ISBN 978-1-4765-3456-5 (paperback)
ISBN 978-1-4765-3452-7 (eBook PDF)
1. Space flight—Juvenile literature. 2. Astronauts—Juvenile literature. 3. Space flight—Comic books, strips, etc. 4. Astronauts—Comic books, strips, etc. 5. Graphic novels. I. Pop Art Properties, illustrator. II. Title.
TL793.B523 2014
629.4'1—dc23 2013003122

Designer
Ted Williams

Cover Artist
Marcelo Baez

Media Researcher
Wanda Winch

Production Specialist
Eric Manske

Editor
Christopher L. Harbo

Photo Credits: NASA: 16, 21

Printed in the United States 6006

TABLE OF CONTENTS

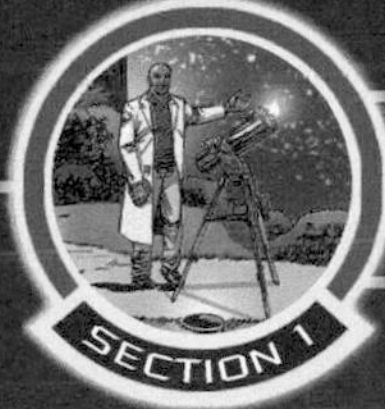
SECTION 1

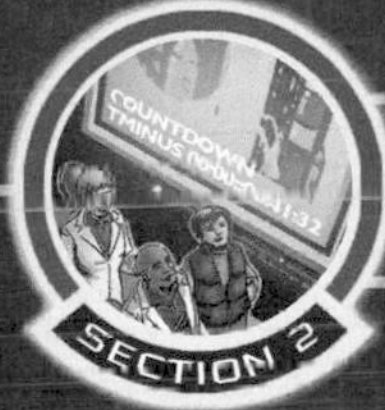
COUNTDOWN
SECTION 2

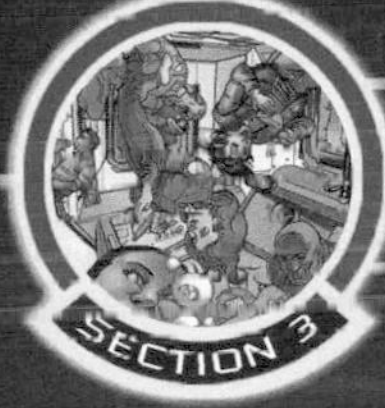
SECTION 3

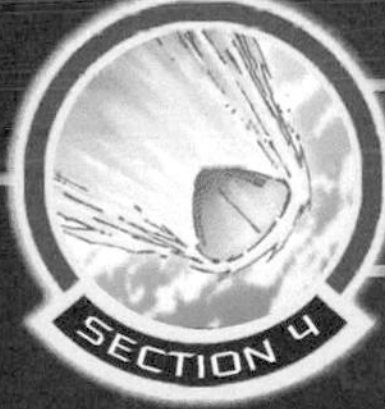
SECTION 4

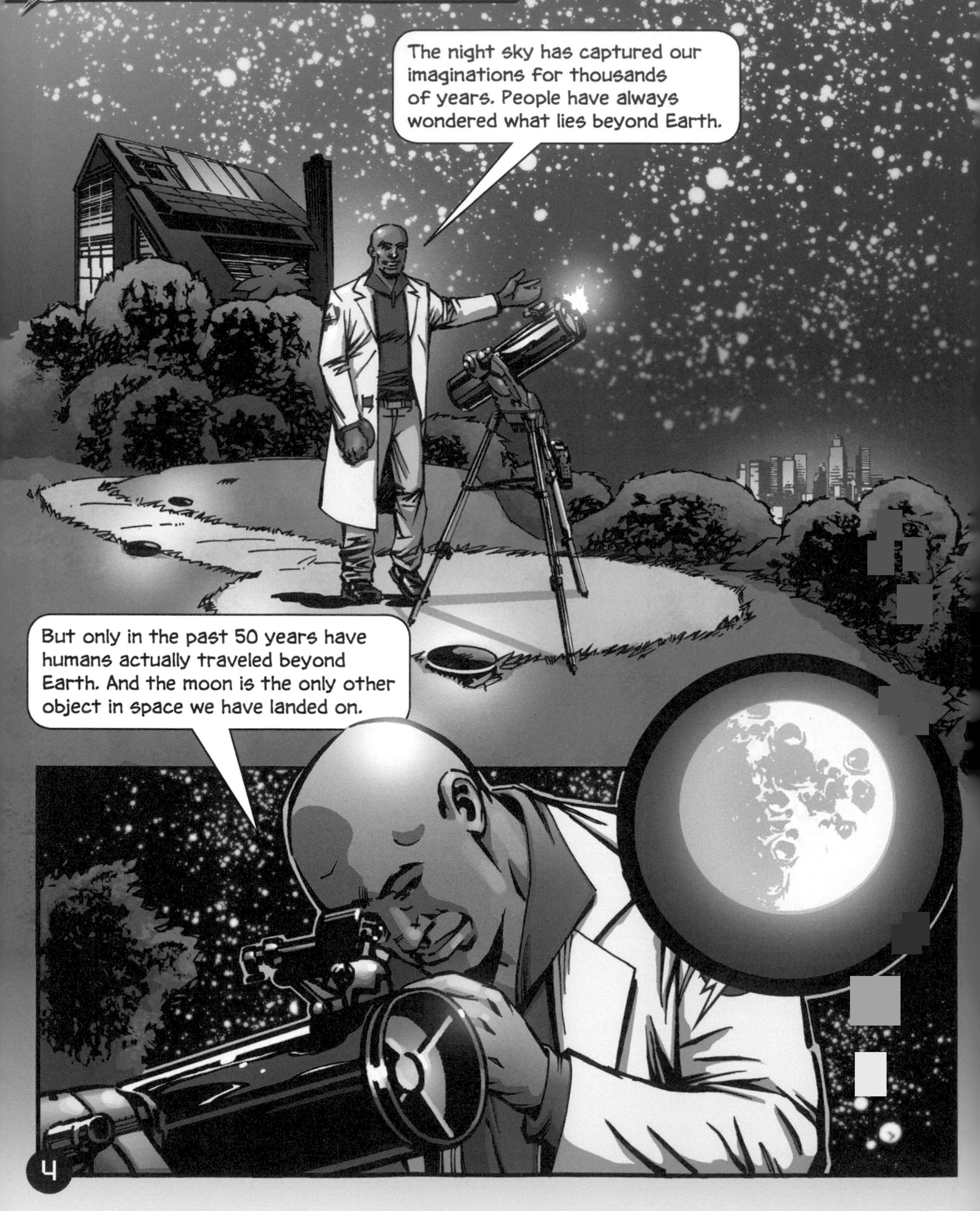
The night sky has captured our imaginations for thousands of years. People have always wondered what lies beyond Earth.
But only in the past 50 years have humans actually traveled beyond Earth. And the moon is the only other object in space we have landed on.

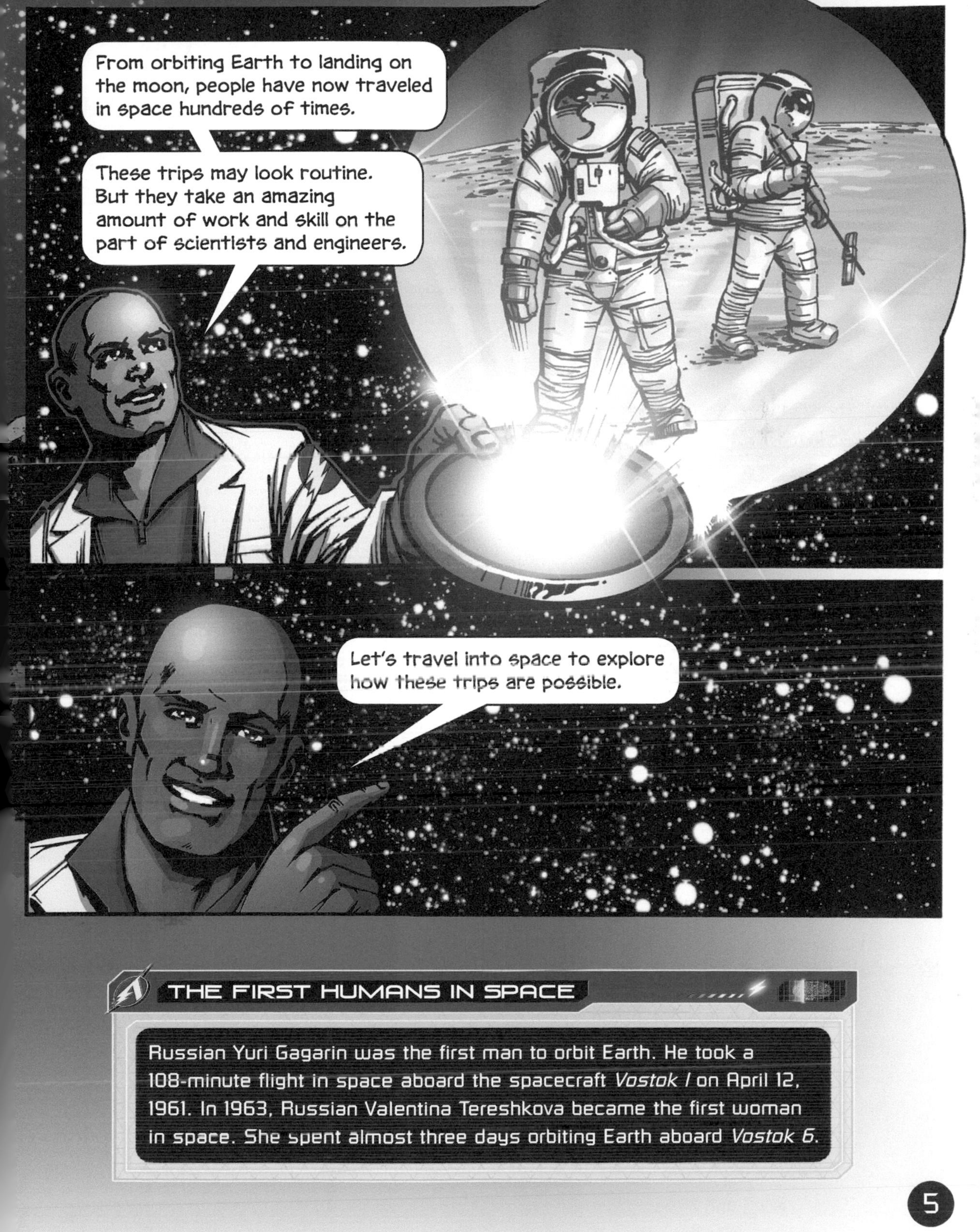

From orbiting Earth to landing on the moon, people have now traveled in space hundreds of times.
These trips may look routine. But they take an amazing amount of work and skill on the part of scientists and engineers.
Let's travel into space to explore how these trips are possible.

THE FIRST HUMANS IN SPACE

Russian Yuri Gagarin was the first man to orbit Earth. He took a 108-minute flight in space aboard the spacecraft *Vostok I* on April 12, 1961. In 1963, Russian Valentina Tereshkova became the first woman in space. She spent almost three days orbiting Earth aboard *Vostok 6*.

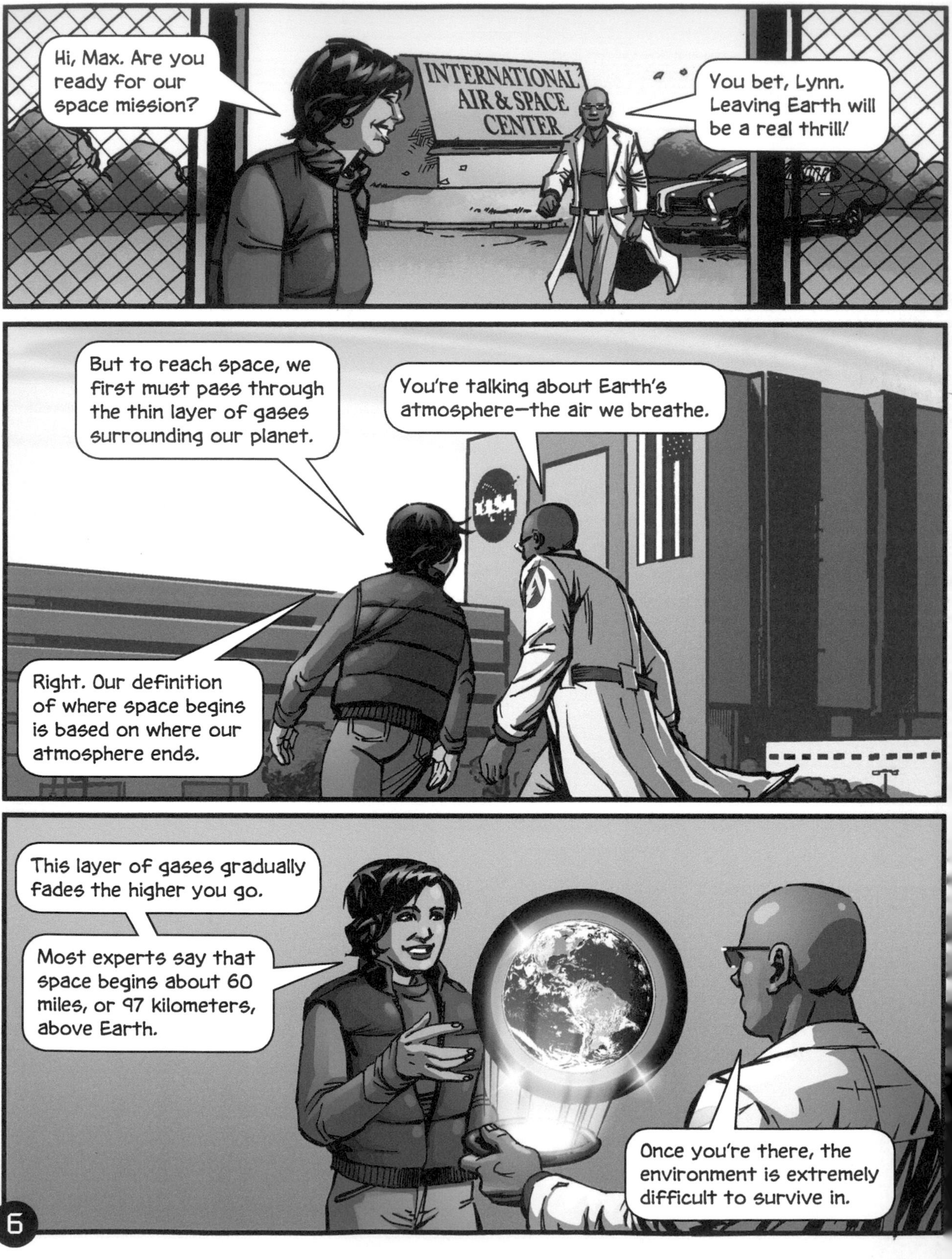
Hi, Max. Are you ready for our space mission?
INTERNATIONAL AIR & SPACE CENTER
You bet, Lynn. Leaving Earth will be a real thrill!
But to reach space, we first must pass through the thin layer of gases surrounding our planet.
You're talking about Earth's atmosphere—the air we breathe.
Right. Our definition of where space begins is based on where our atmosphere ends.
This layer of gases gradually fades the higher you go.
Most experts say that space begins about 60 miles, or 97 kilometers, above Earth.
Once you're there, the environment is extremely difficult to survive in.

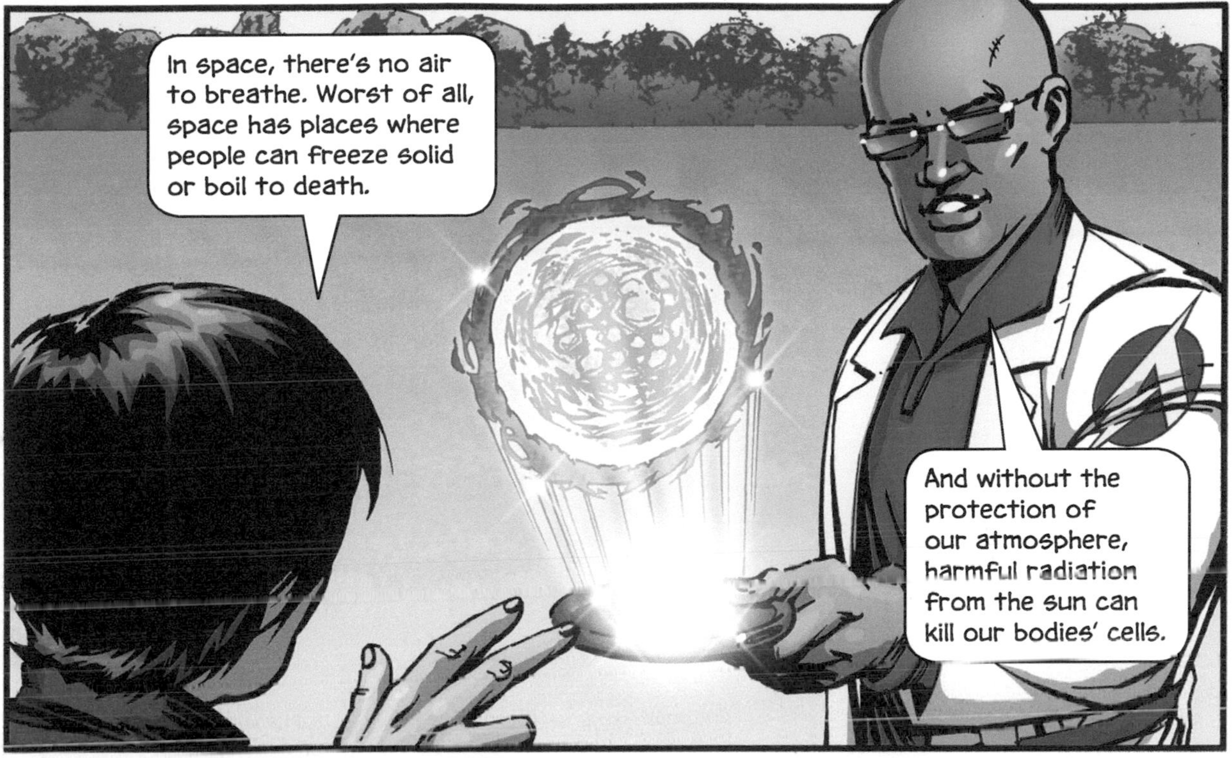
In space, there's no air to breathe. Worst of all, space has places where people can freeze solid or boil to death.
And without the protection of our atmosphere, harmful radiation from the sun can kill our bodies' cells.

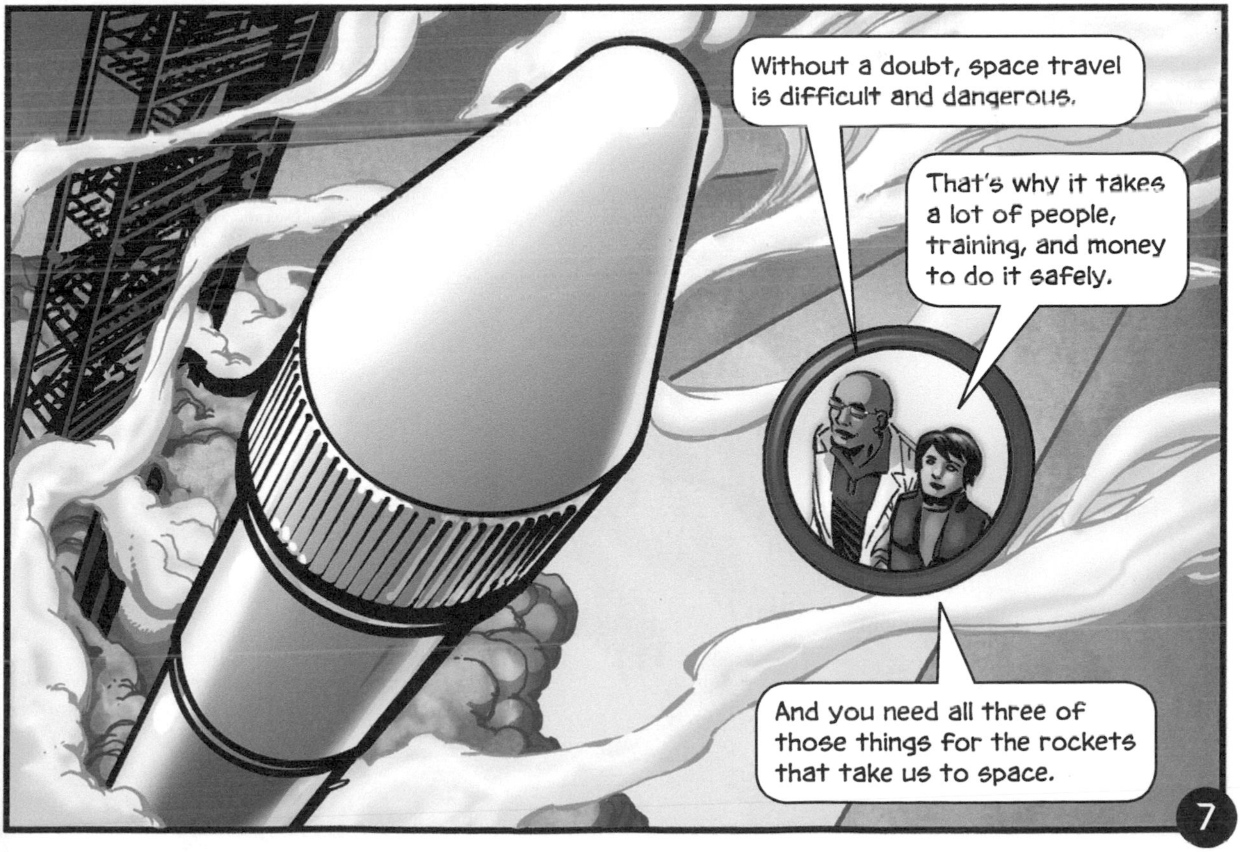
Without a doubt, space travel is difficult and dangerous.
That's why it takes a lot of people, training, and money to do it safely.
And you need all three of those things for the rockets that take us to space.

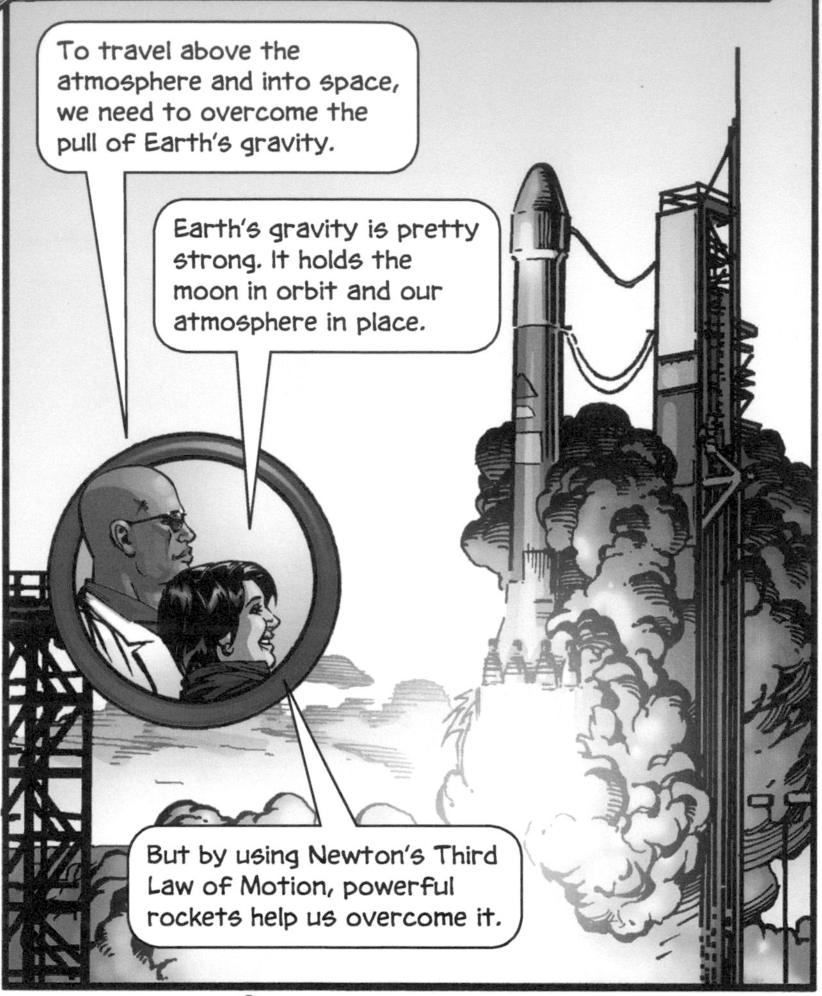
To travel above the atmosphere and into space, we need to overcome the pull of Earth's gravity.
Earth's gravity is pretty strong. It holds the moon in orbit and our atmosphere in place.
But by using Newton's Third Law of Motion, powerful rockets help us overcome it.

It's the Law

More than 300 years ago, English scientist Isaac Newton came up with three simple laws that describe how forces make things move. His third law is probably the most famous. It says that for every action there is an equal and opposite reaction. By actions, Newton meant forces. Rockets aren't the only things that use this law. You can see it in action by blowing up a balloon and then letting it go. The force of the air coming out of the balloon is equal to the force of the balloon whizzing around you.

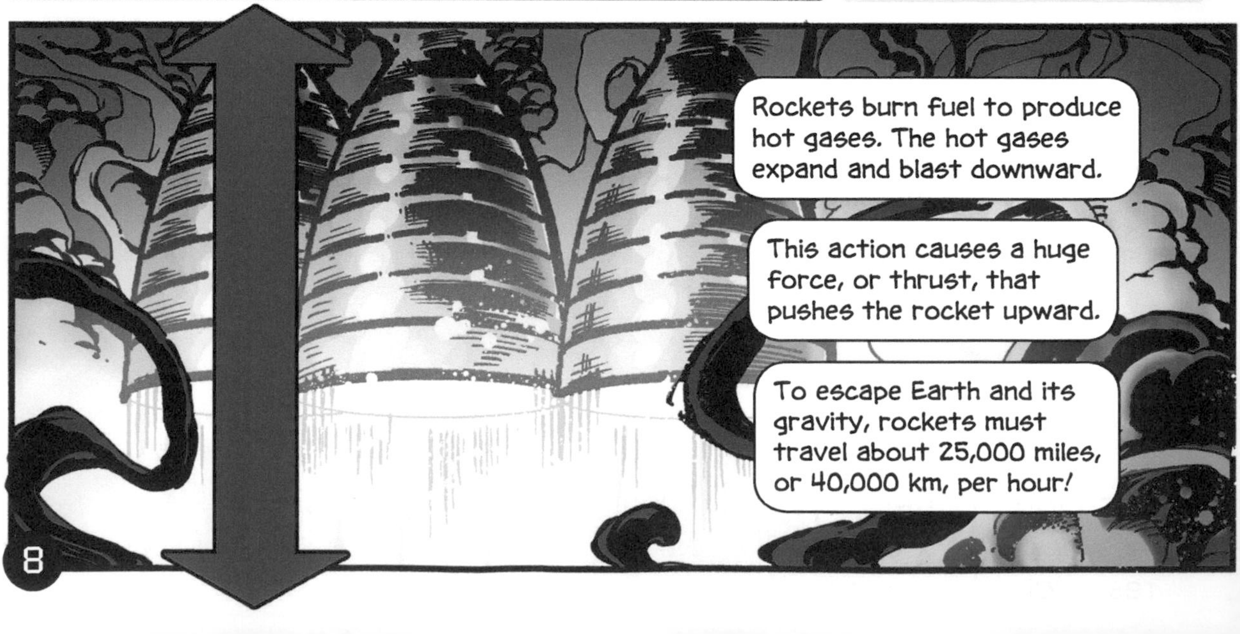
Rockets burn fuel to produce hot gases. The hot gases expand and blast downward.
This action causes a huge force, or thrust, that pushes the rocket upward.
To escape Earth and its gravity, rockets must travel about 25,000 miles, or 40,000 km, per hour!

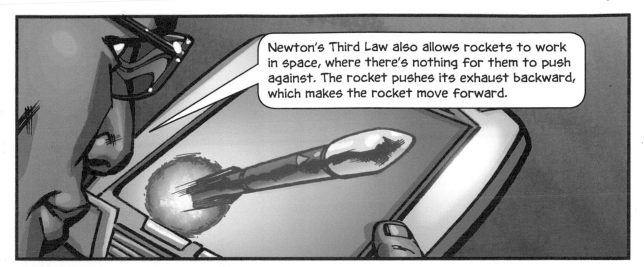

Newton's Third Law also allows rockets to work in space, where there's nothing for them to push against. The rocket pushes its exhaust backward, which makes the rocket move forward.

Rockets come in many sizes, and some are more powerful than others. Heavy lift rockets are among the most powerful. They can send people to the moon and beyond.

Our rocket to the *International Space Station* is going to launch from this spaceport too. It's so huge that we can get a better look at it from the air.

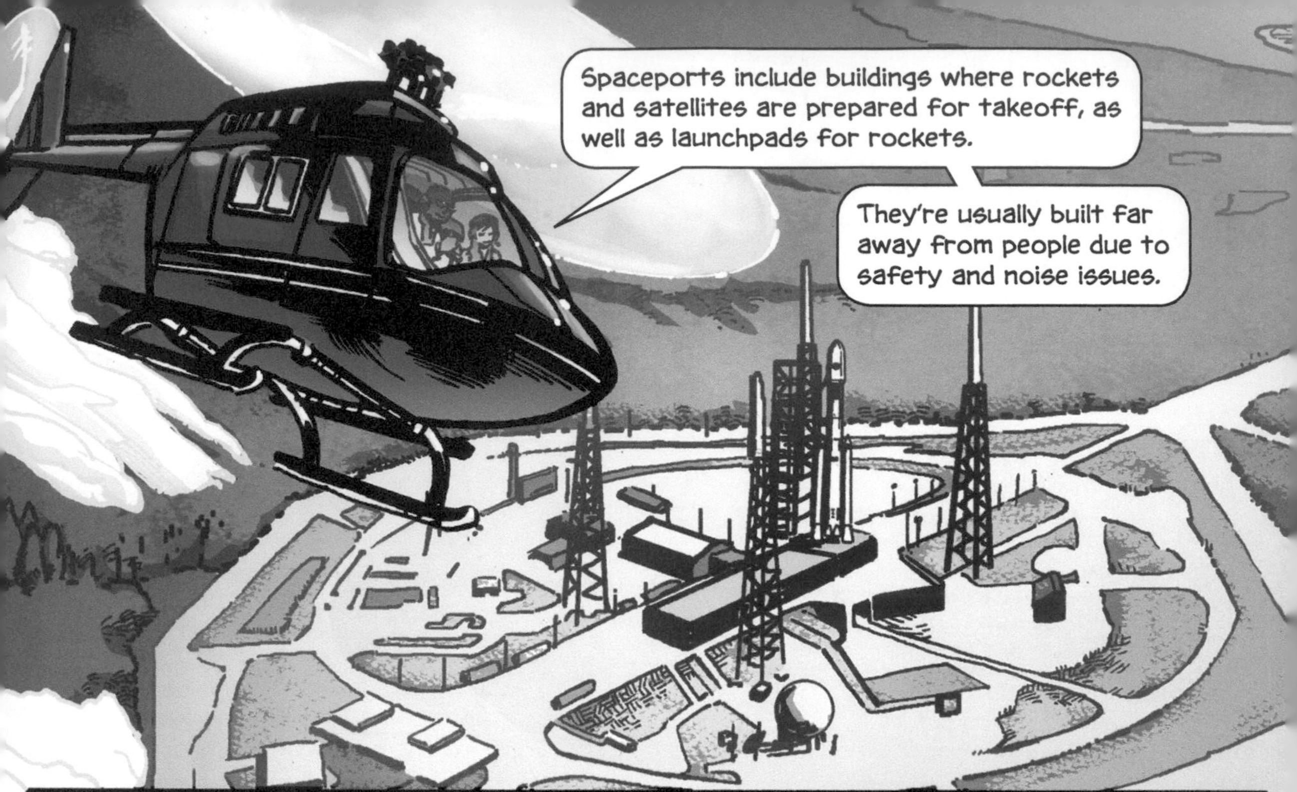
Spaceports include buildings where rockets and satellites are prepared for takeoff, as well as launchpads for rockets.
They're usually built far away from people due to safety and noise issues.

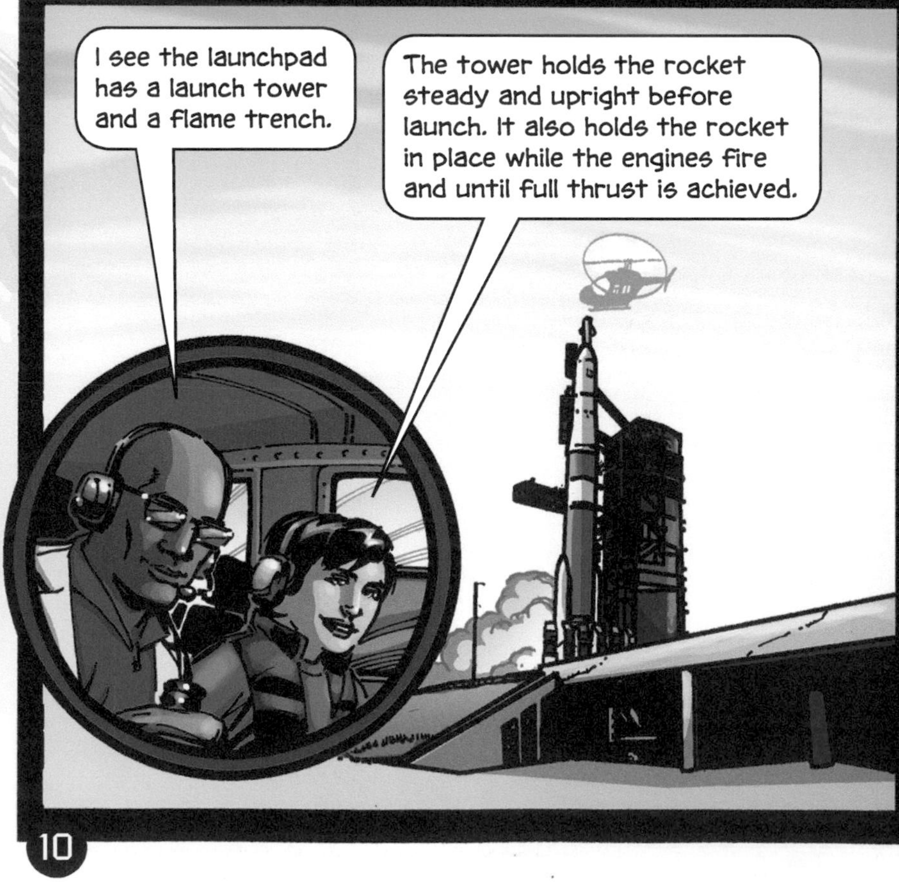
I see the launchpad has a launch tower and a flame trench.
The tower holds the rocket steady and upright before launch. It also holds the rocket in place while the engines fire and until full thrust is achieved.

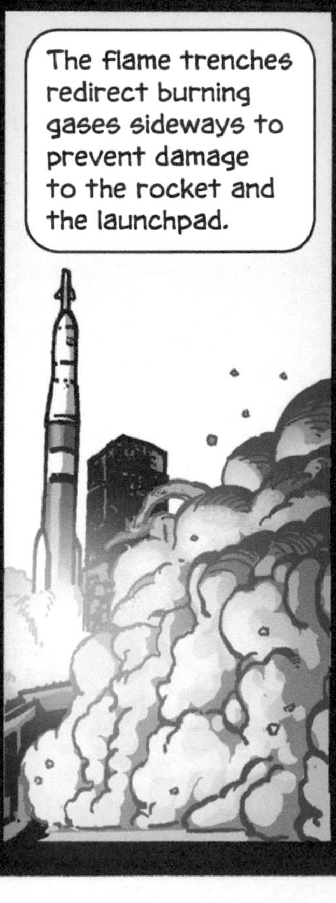
The flame trenches redirect burning gases sideways to prevent damage to the rocket and the launchpad.

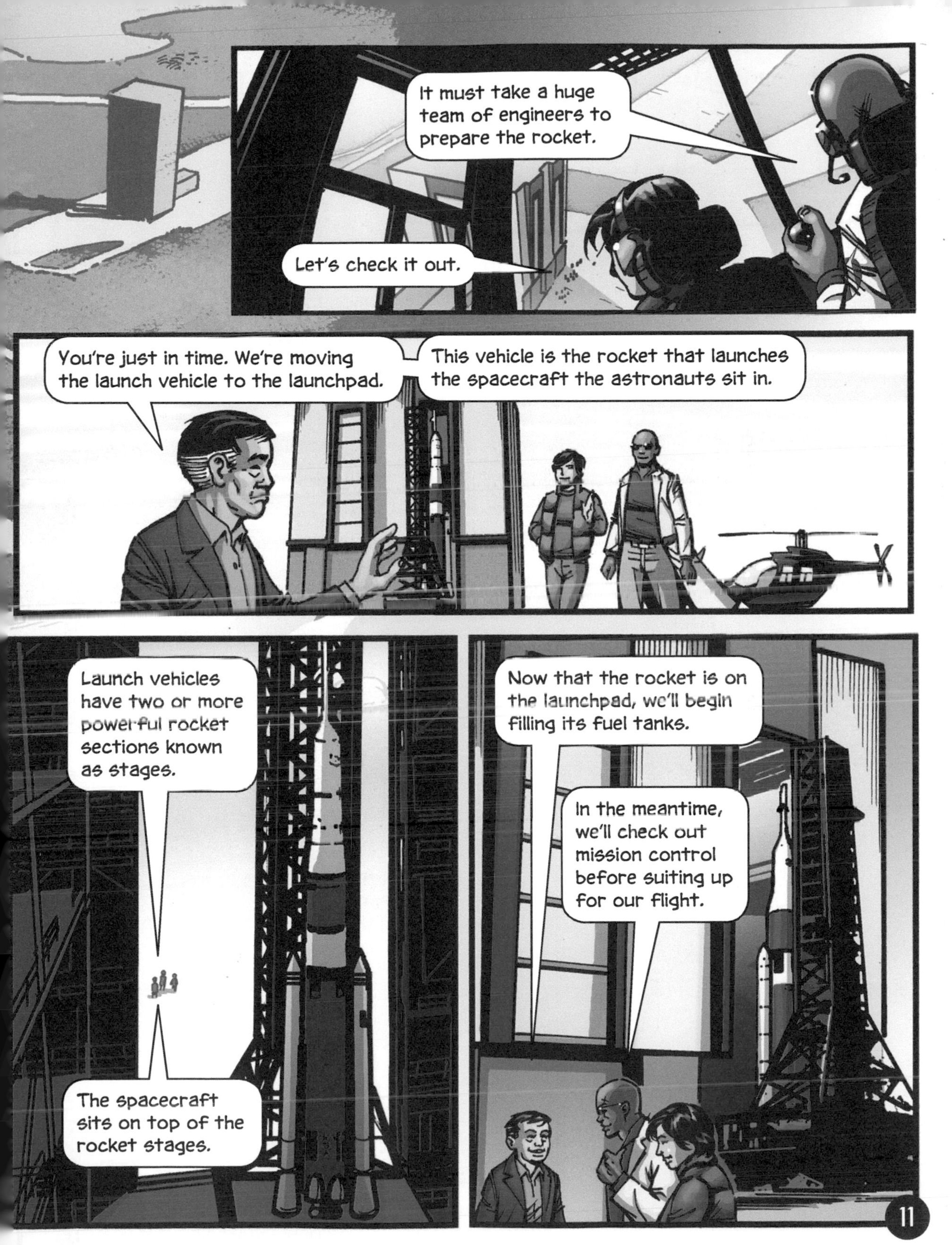

It must take a huge team of engineers to prepare the rocket.
Let's check it out.
You're just in time. We're moving the launch vehicle to the launchpad.
This vehicle is the rocket that launches the spacecraft the astronauts sit in.
Launch vehicles have two or more powerful rocket sections known as stages.
The spacecraft sits on top of the rocket stages.
Now that the rocket is on the launchpad, we'll begin filling its fuel tanks.
In the meantime, we'll check out mission control before suiting up for our flight.

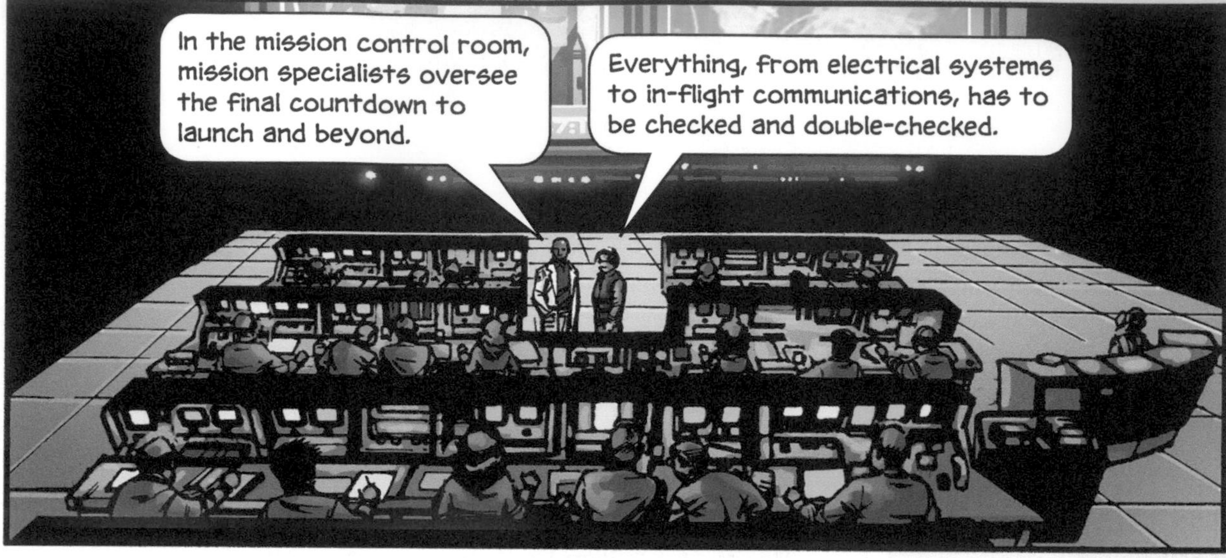
In the mission control room, mission specialists oversee the final countdown to launch and beyond.
Everything, from electrical systems to in-flight communications, has to be checked and double-checked.

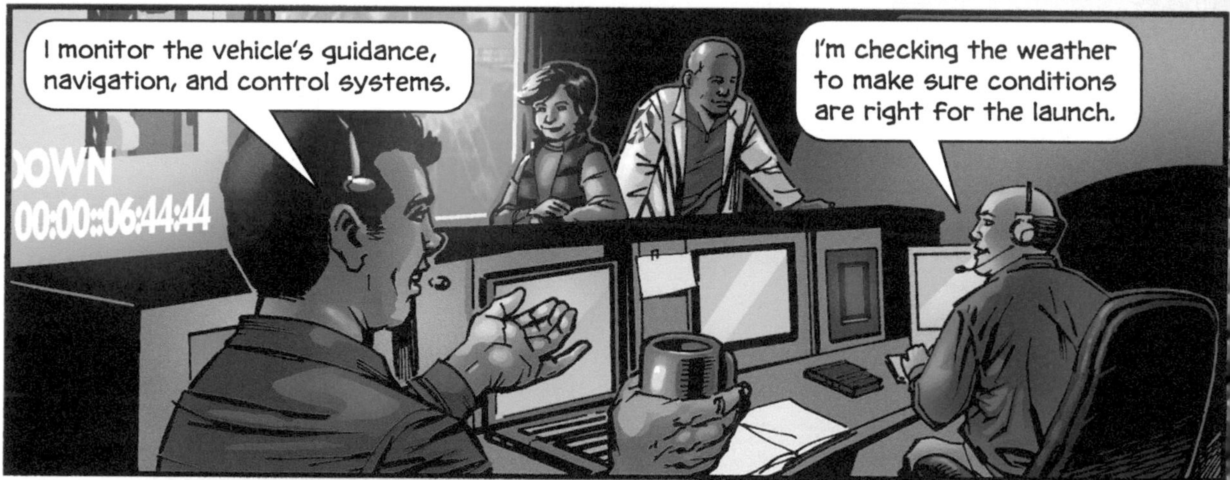
I monitor the vehicle's guidance, navigation, and control systems.
I'm checking the weather to make sure conditions are right for the launch.
00:00::06:44:44

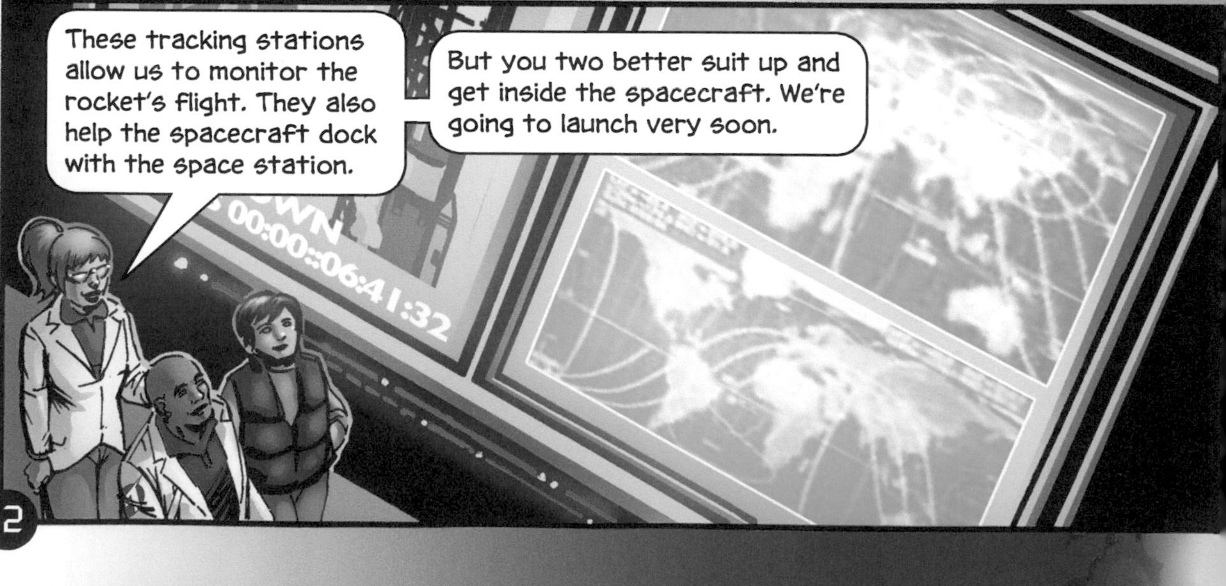
These tracking stations allow us to monitor the rocket's flight. They also help the spacecraft dock with the space station.
But you two better suit up and get inside the spacecraft. We're going to launch very soon.
00:00::06:41:32

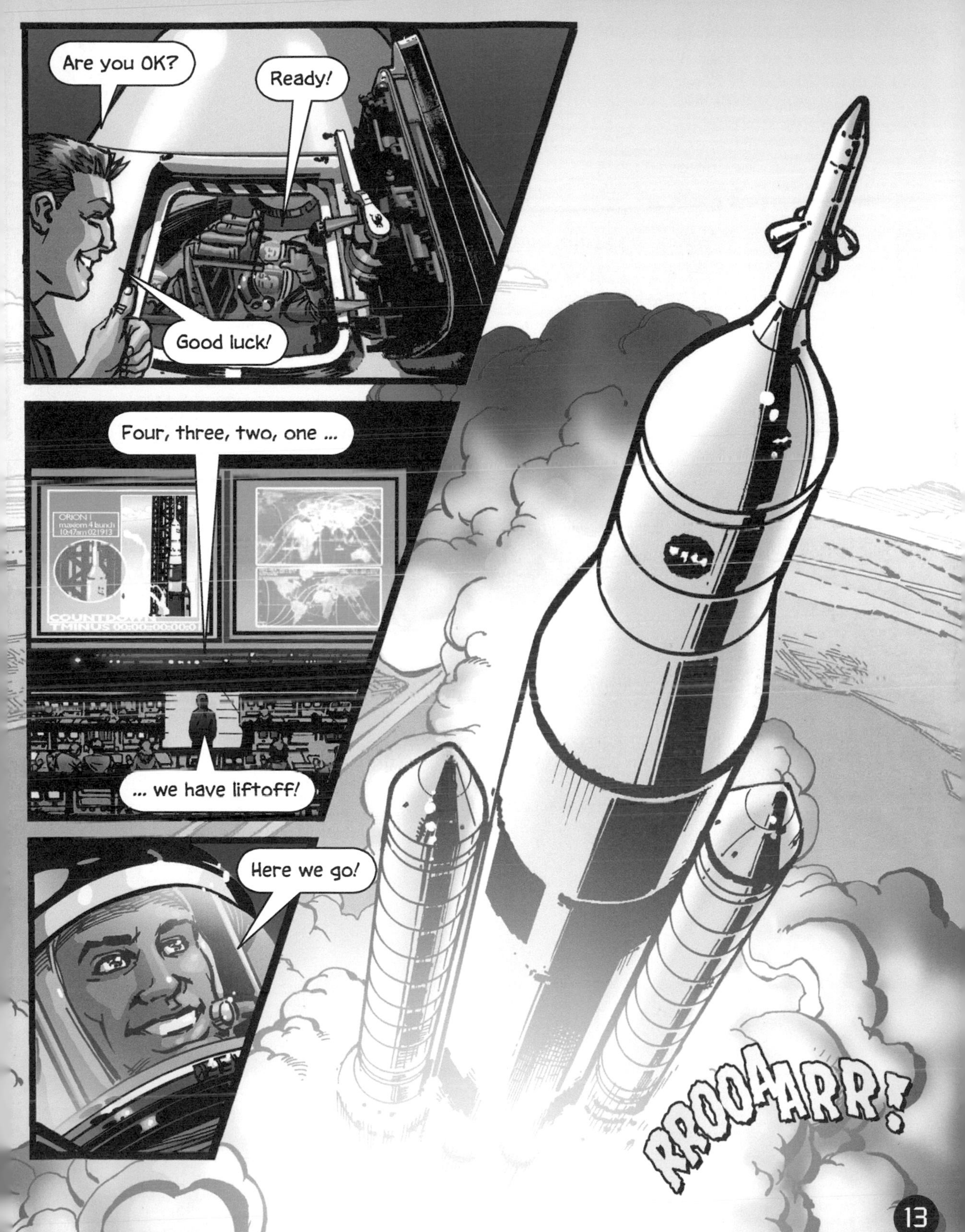
Are you OK?
Ready!
Good luck!
Four, three, two, one ...
COUNTDOWN
... we have liftoff!
Here we go!
RROOAARR!

Launching a craft into space is a multi-stage process. First, thrust causes the launch vehicle to rise above the launchpad.

A few minutes later, the rocket's first stage falls away when its fuel has been used up.

Then the rocket's second stage fires.

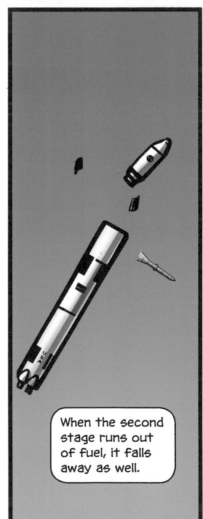

When the second stage runs out of fuel, it falls away as well.

Then the spacecraft reaches orbit.

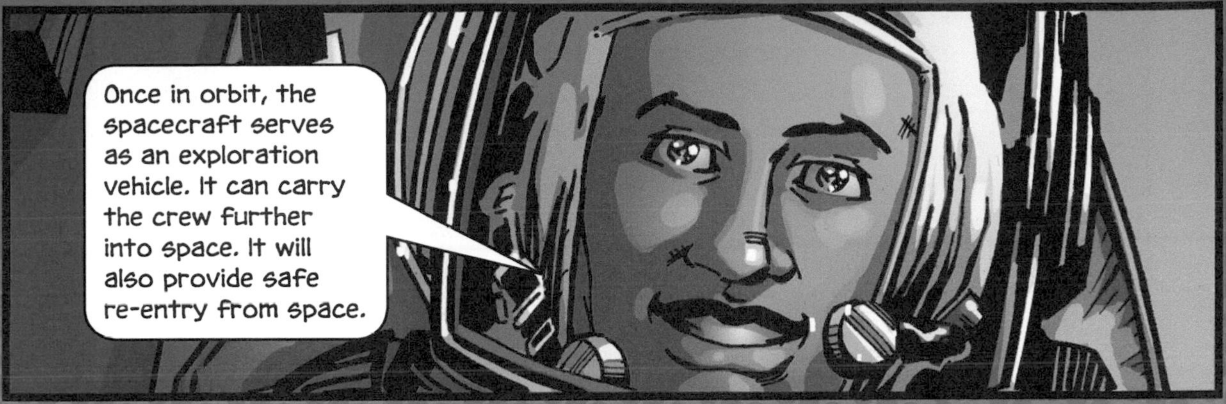
Once in orbit, the spacecraft serves as an exploration vehicle. It can carry the crew further into space. It will also provide safe re-entry from space.

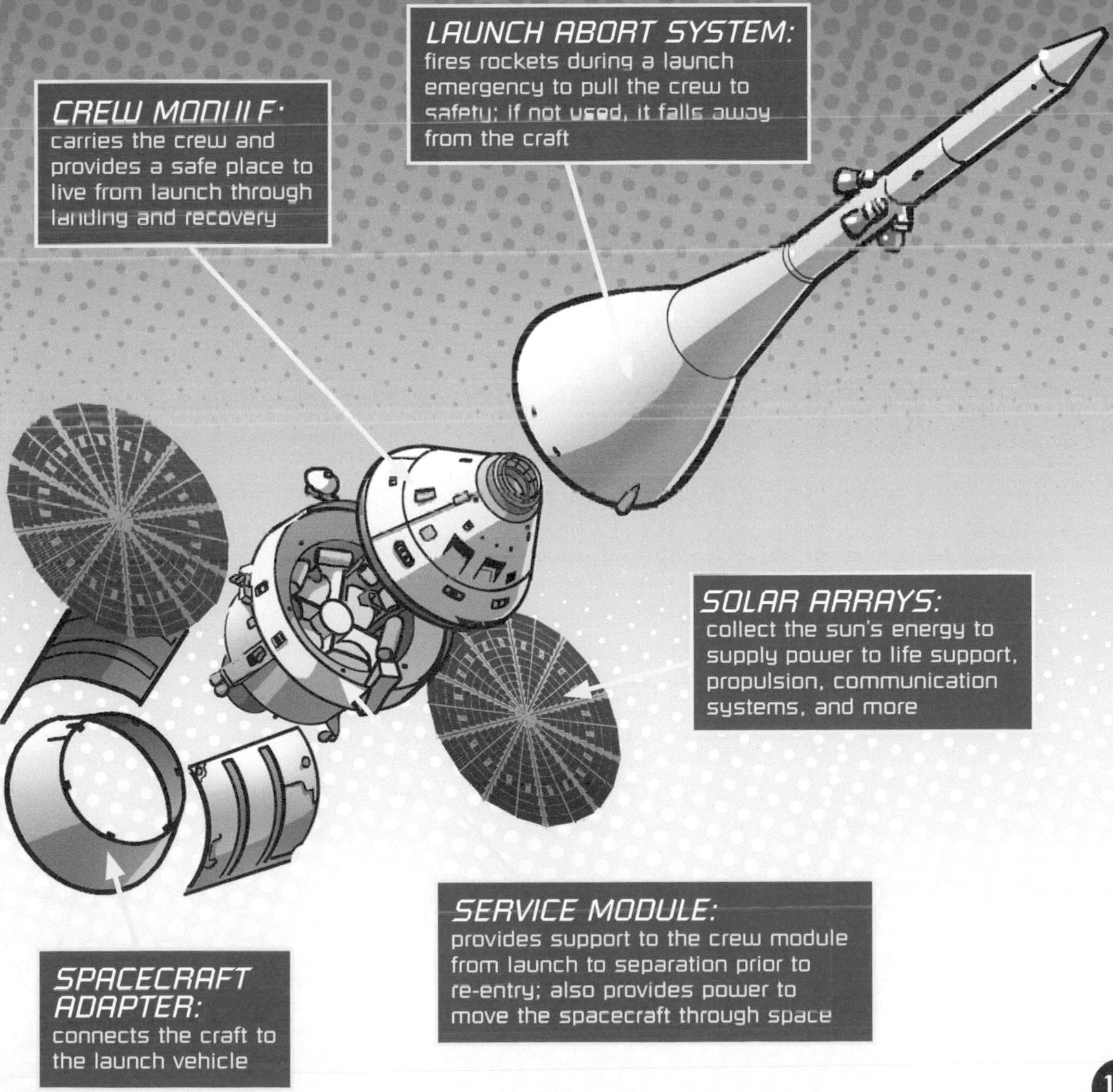
LAUNCH ABORT SYSTEM:
fires rockets during a launch emergency to pull the crew to safety; if not used, it falls away from the craft
CREW MODULE:
carries the crew and provides a safe place to live from launch through landing and recovery
SOLAR ARRAYS:
collect the sun's energy to supply power to life support, propulsion, communication systems, and more
SERVICE MODULE:
provides support to the crew module from launch to separation prior to re-entry; also provides power to move the spacecraft through space
SPACECRAFT ADAPTER:
connects the craft to the launch vehicle

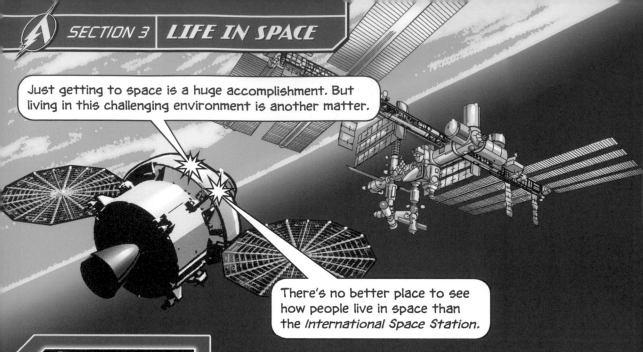

Just getting to space is a huge accomplishment. But living in this challenging environment is another matter.

There's no better place to see how people live in space than the *International Space Station*.

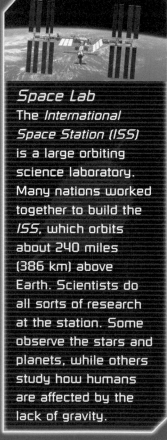

Space Lab
The *International Space Station* (ISS) is a large orbiting science laboratory. Many nations worked together to build the *ISS*, which orbits about 240 miles (386 km) above Earth. Scientists do all sorts of research at the station. Some observe the stars and planets, while others study how humans are affected by the lack of gravity.

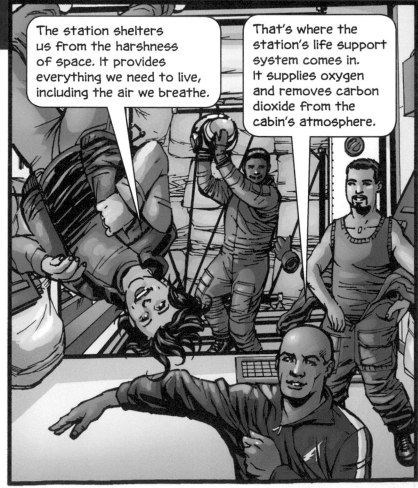

The station shelters us from the harshness of space. It provides everything we need to live, including the air we breathe.

That's where the station's life support system comes in. It supplies oxygen and removes carbon dioxide from the cabin's atmosphere.

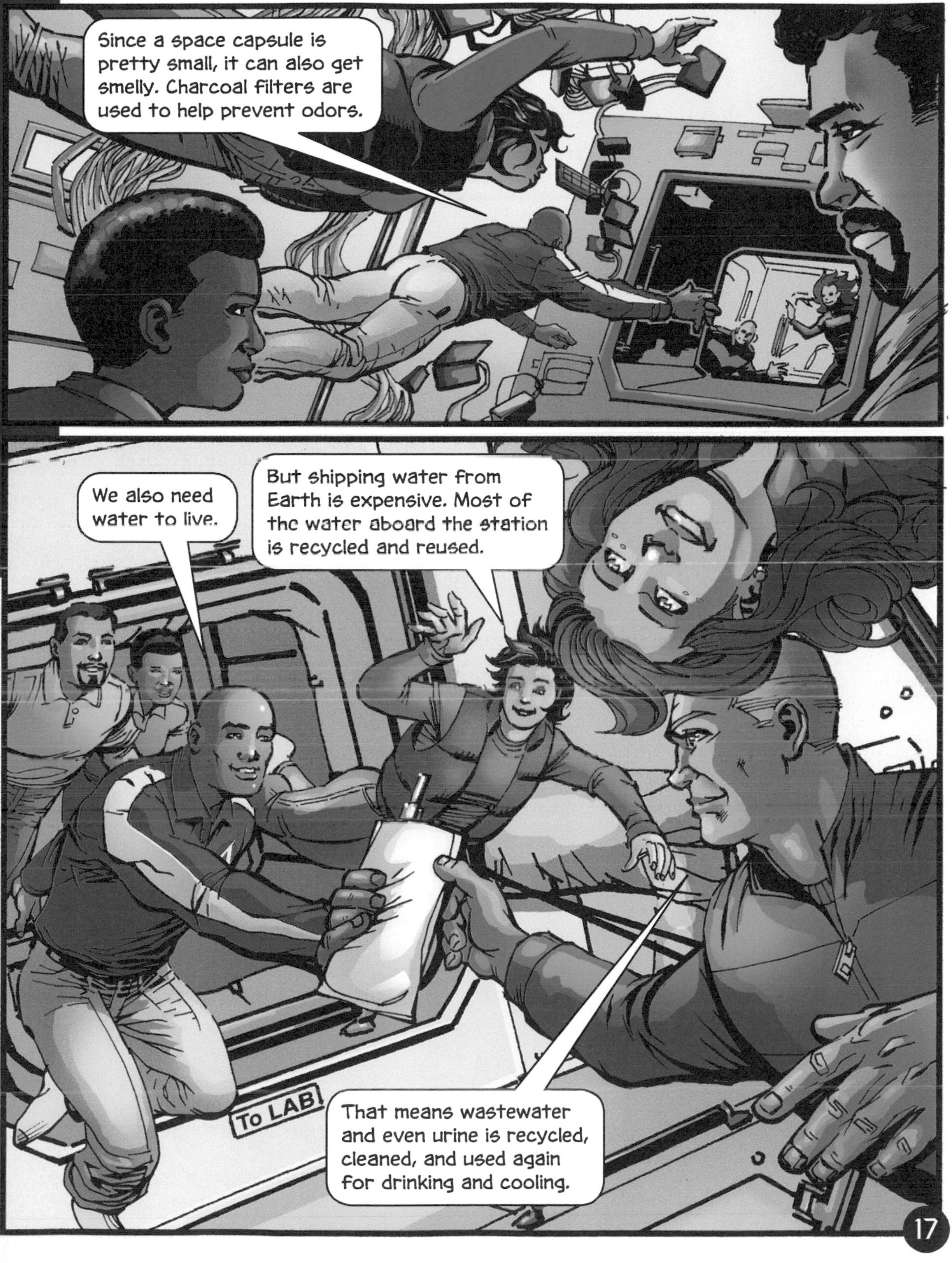
Since a space capsule is pretty small, it can also get smelly. Charcoal filters are used to help prevent odors.
We also need water to live.
But shipping water from Earth is expensive. Most of the water aboard the station is recycled and reused.
To LAB
That means wastewater and even urine is recycled, cleaned, and used again for drinking and cooling.

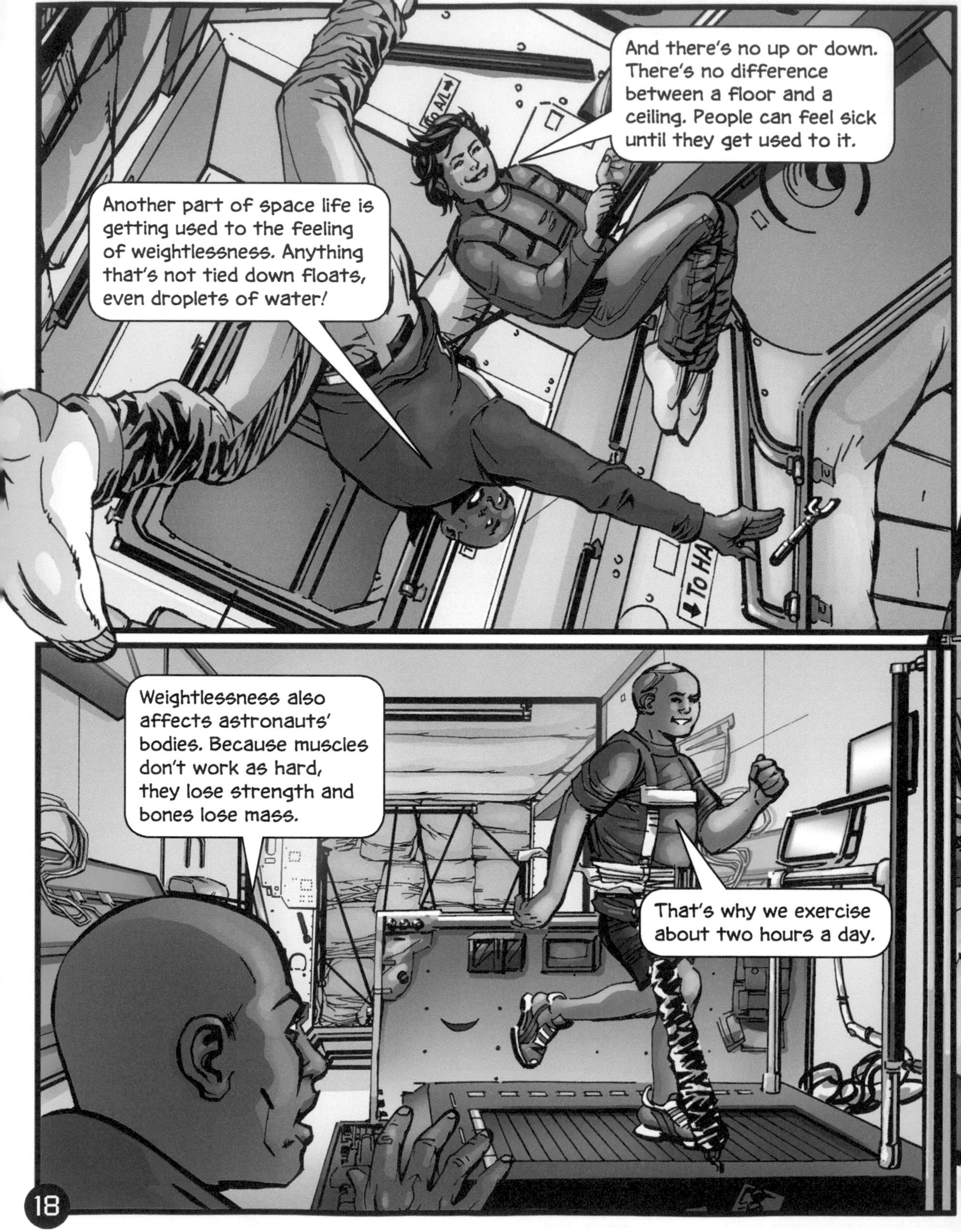
Another part of space life is getting used to the feeling of weightlessness. Anything that's not tied down floats, even droplets of water!
And there's no up or down. There's no difference between a floor and a ceiling. People can feel sick until they get used to it.
To A/L
To HA
Weightlessness also affects astronauts' bodies. Because muscles don't work as hard, they lose strength and bones lose mass.
That's why we exercise about two hours a day.

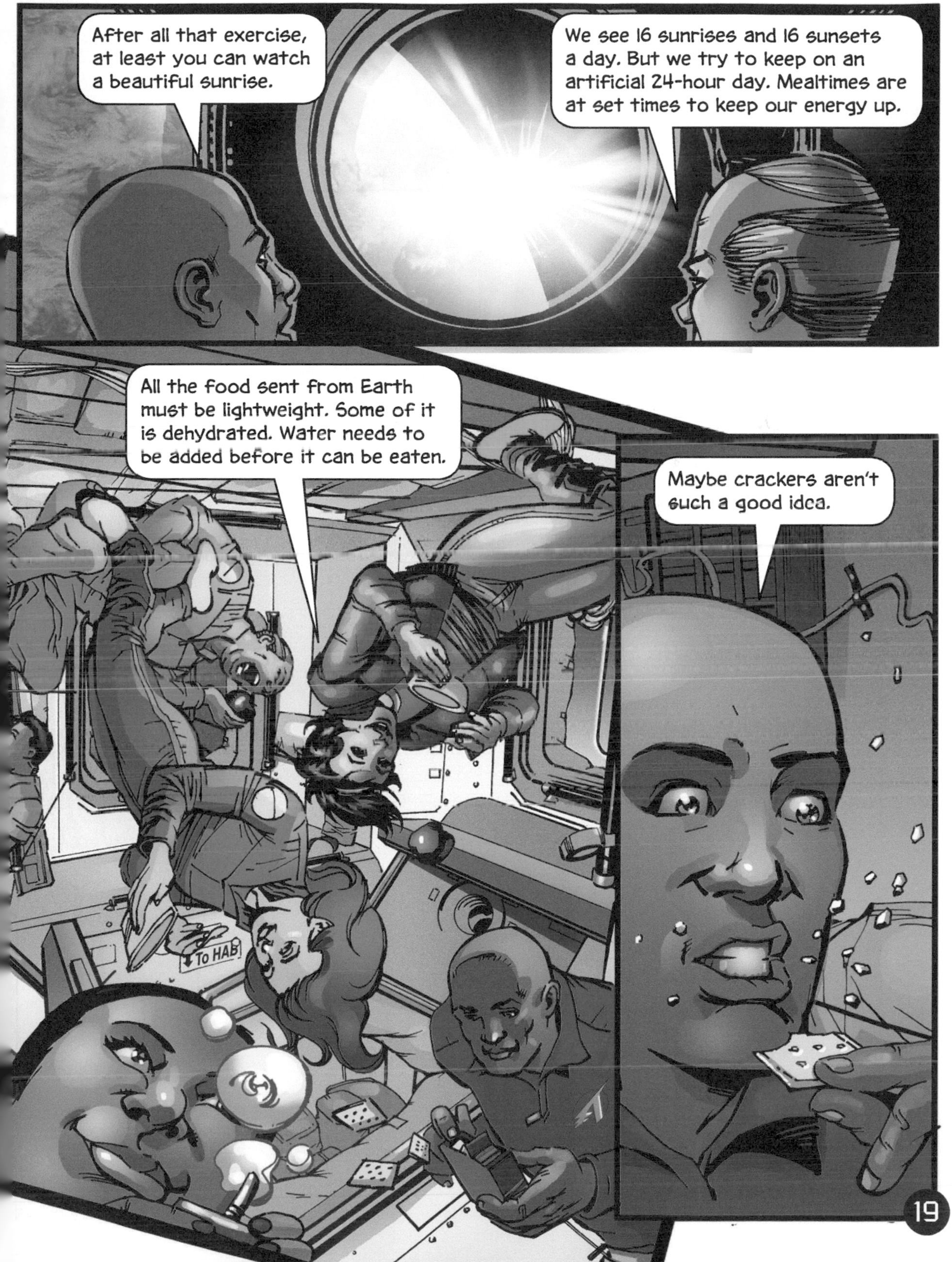
After all that exercise, at least you can watch a beautiful sunrise.
We see 16 sunrises and 16 sunsets a day. But we try to keep on an artificial 24-hour day. Mealtimes are at set times to keep our energy up.
All the food sent from Earth must be lightweight. Some of it is dehydrated. Water needs to be added before it can be eaten.
TO HAB
Maybe crackers aren't such a good idea.

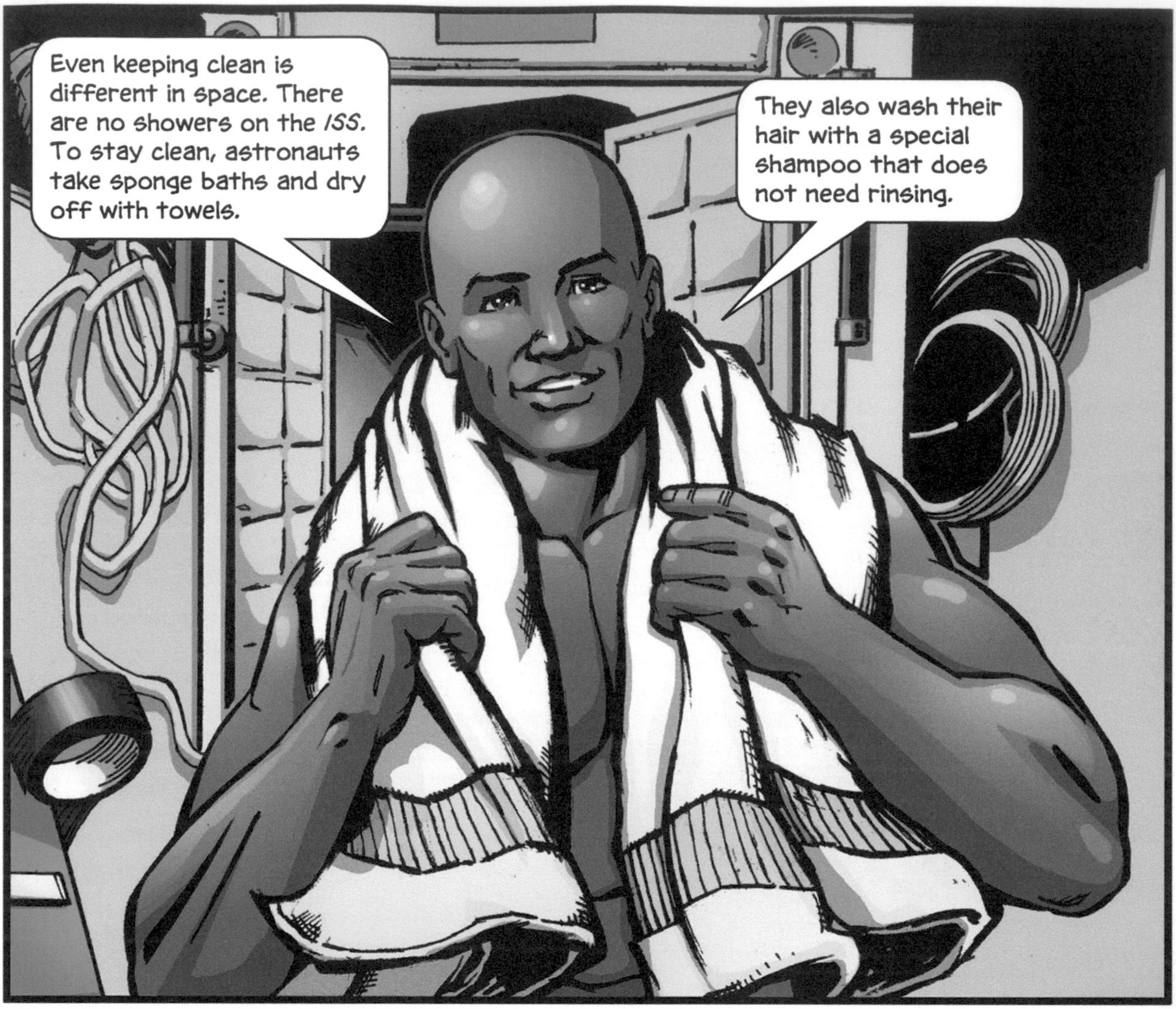
Even keeping clean is different in space. There are no showers on the *ISS*. To stay clean, astronauts take sponge baths and dry off with towels.
They also wash their hair with a special shampoo that does not need rinsing.

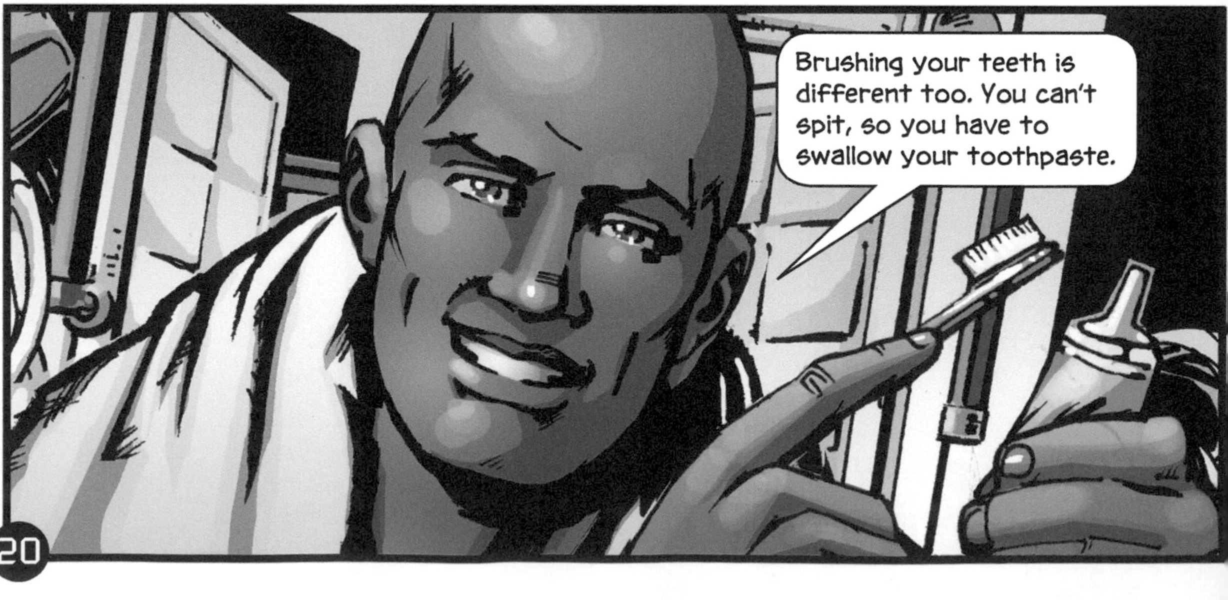
Brushing your teeth is different too. You can't spit, so you have to swallow your toothpaste.

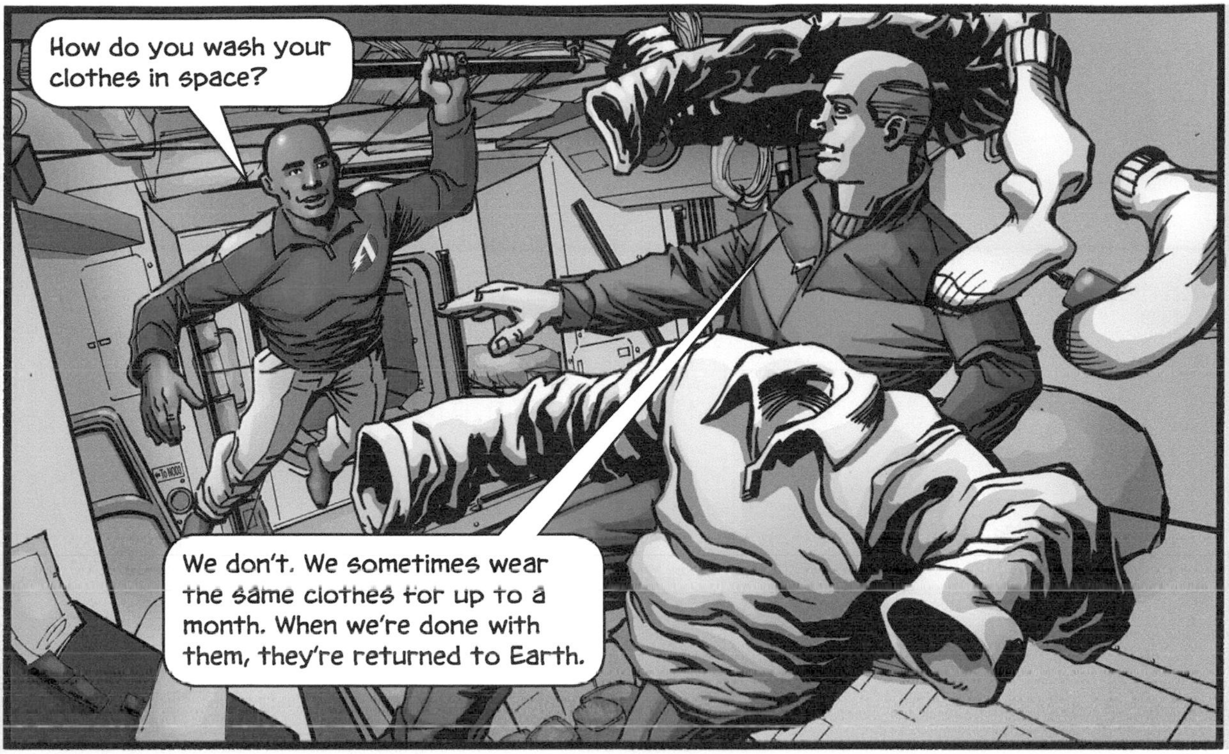
How do you wash your clothes in space?
We don't. We sometimes wear the same clothes for up to a month. When we're done with them, they're returned to Earth.

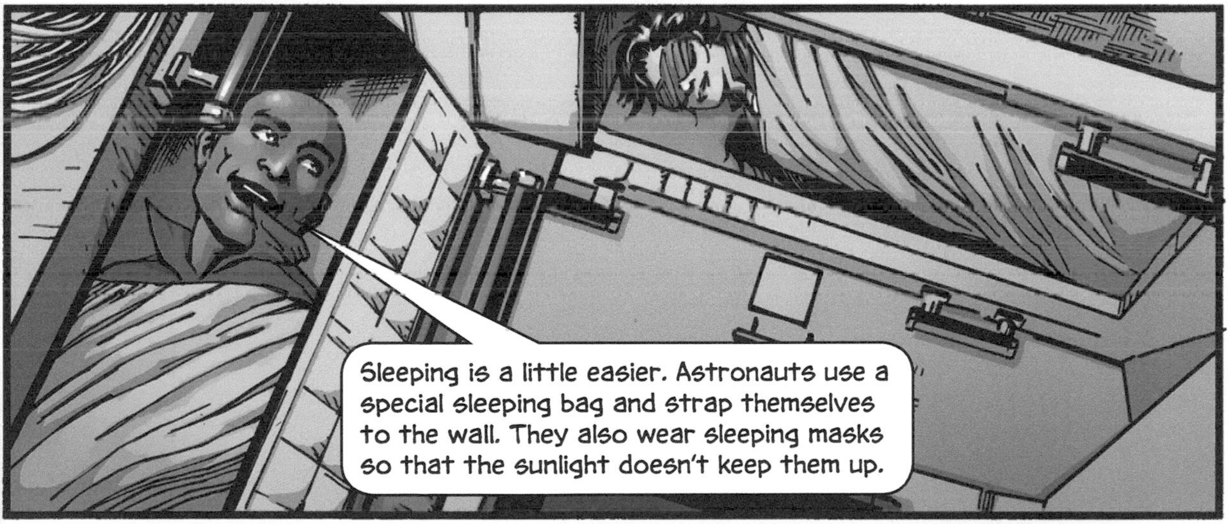
Sleeping is a little easier. Astronauts use a special sleeping bag and strap themselves to the wall. They also wear sleeping masks so that the sunlight doesn't keep them up.

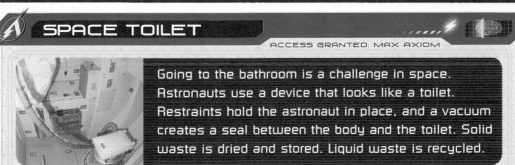

SPACE TOILET

ACCESS GRANTED: MAX AXIOM

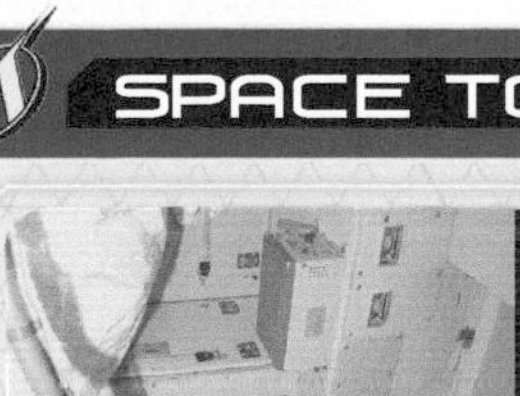

Going to the bathroom is a challenge in space. Astronauts use a device that looks like a toilet. Restraints hold the astronaut in place, and a vacuum creates a seal between the body and the toilet. Solid waste is dried and stored. Liquid waste is recycled.

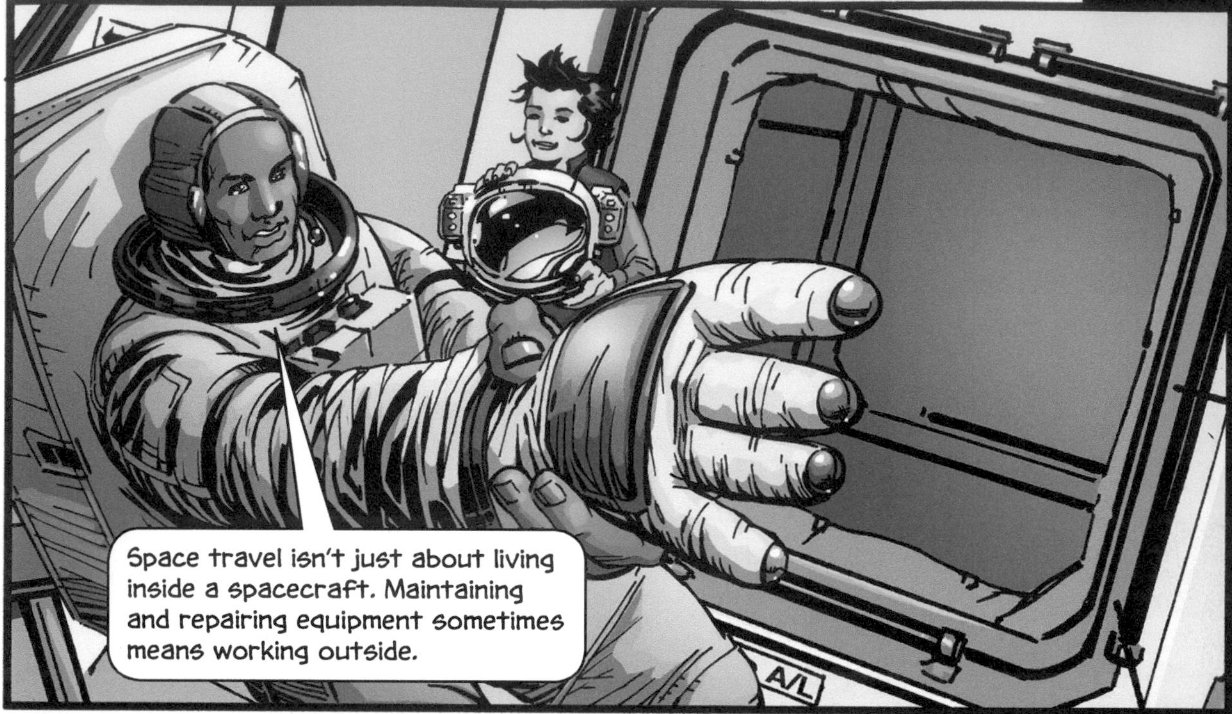
Space travel isn't just about living inside a spacecraft. Maintaining and repairing equipment sometimes means working outside.
A/L

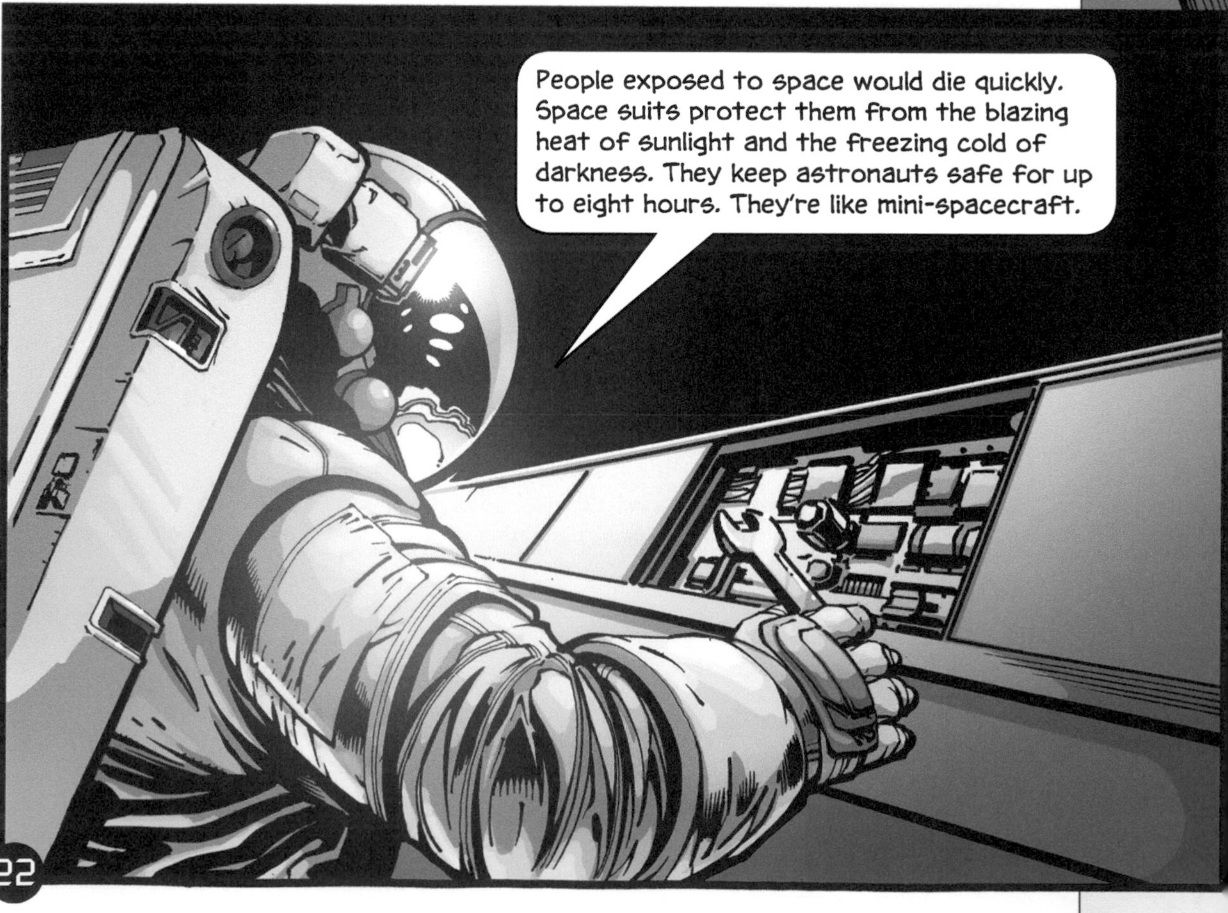
People exposed to space would die quickly. Space suits protect them from the blazing heat of sunlight and the freezing cold of darkness. They keep astronauts safe for up to eight hours. They're like mini-spacecraft.

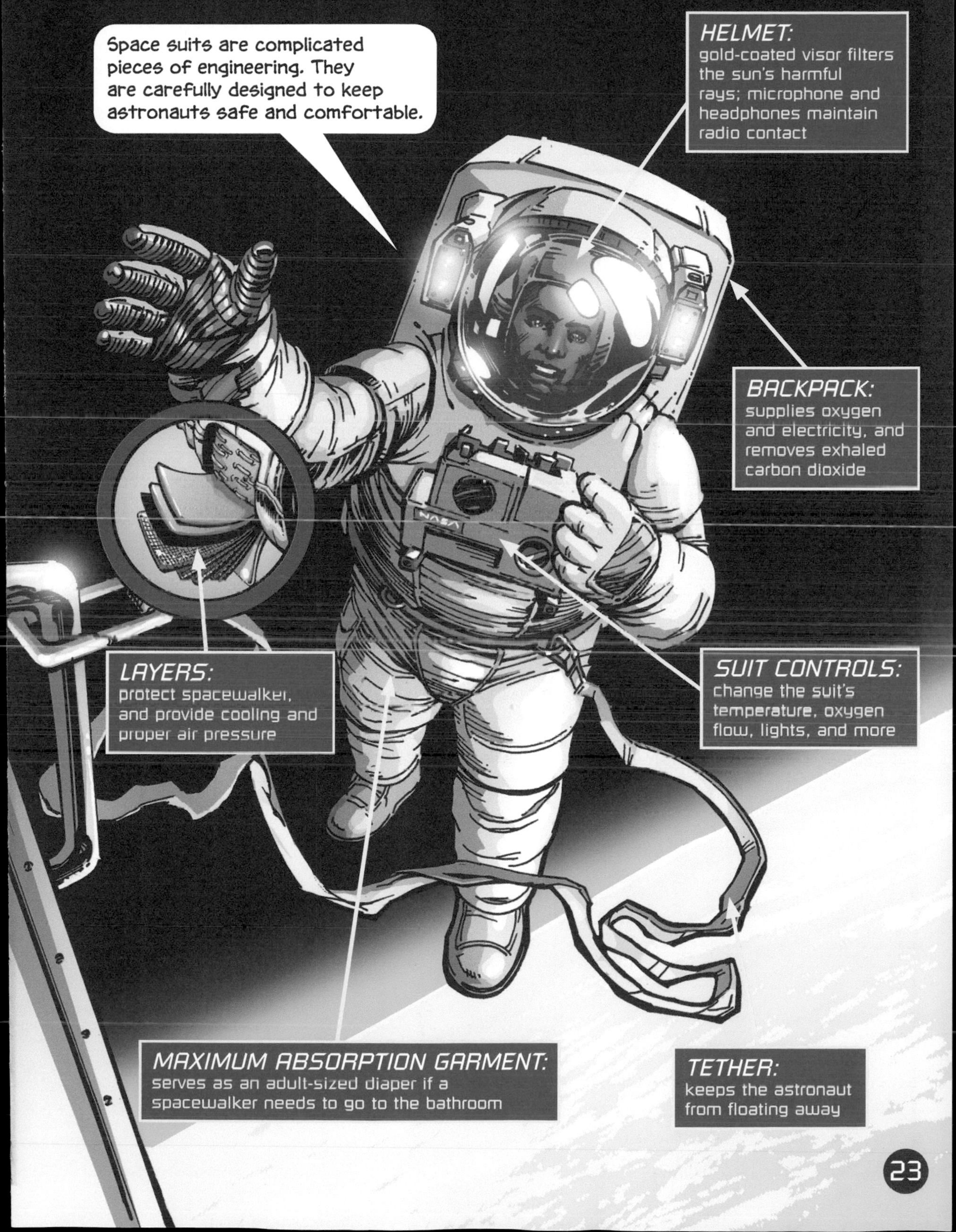
Space suits are complicated pieces of engineering. They are carefully designed to keep astronauts safe and comfortable.
HELMET: gold-coated visor filters the sun's harmful rays; microphone and headphones maintain radio contact
BACKPACK: supplies oxygen and electricity, and removes exhaled carbon dioxide
LAYERS: protect spacewalker, and provide cooling and proper air pressure
SUIT CONTROLS: change the suit's temperature, oxygen flow, lights, and more
NASA
MAXIMUM ABSORPTION GARMENT: serves as an adult-sized diaper if a spacewalker needs to go to the bathroom
TETHER: keeps the astronaut from floating away

SECTION 4 DOWN TO EARTH

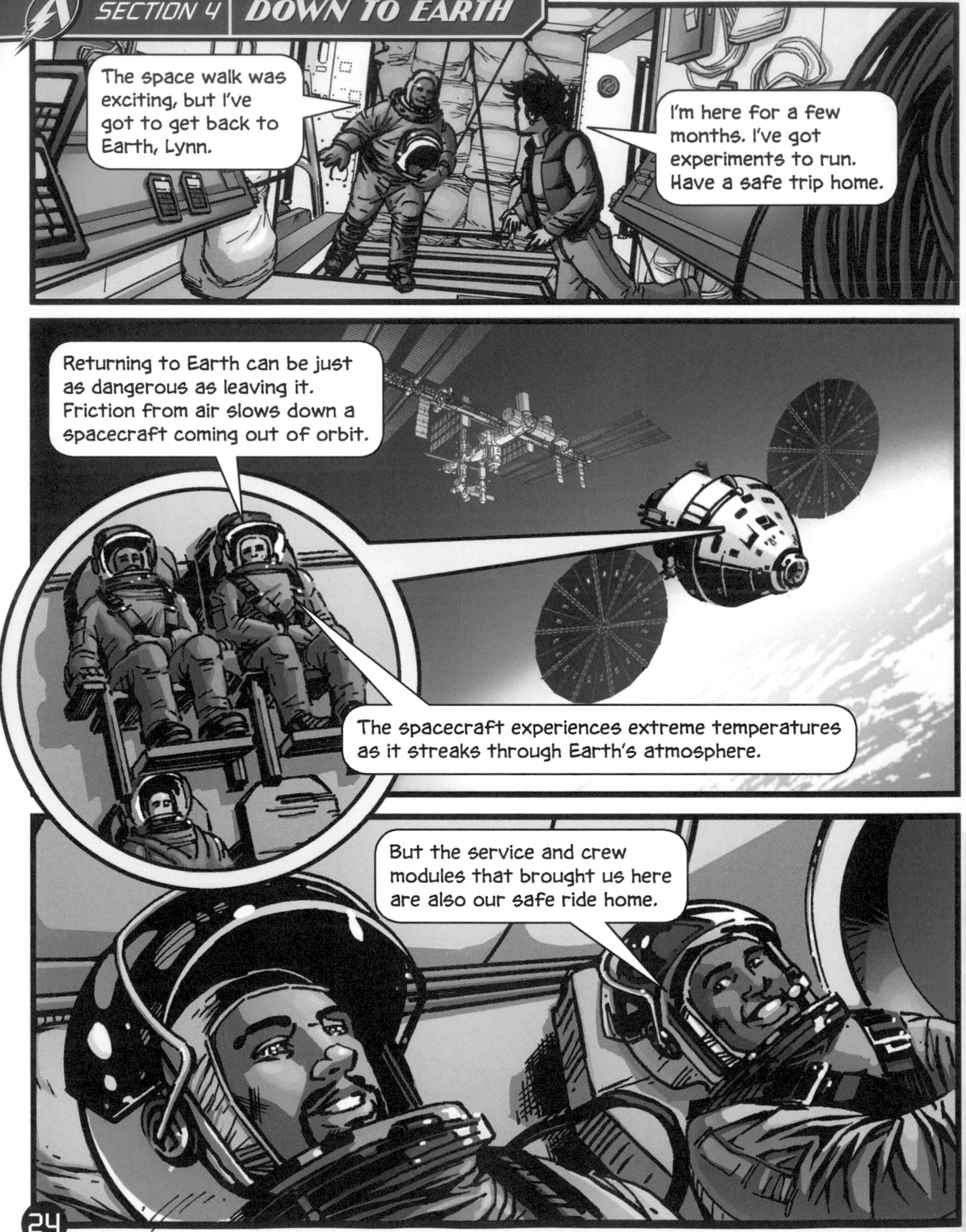

The space walk was exciting, but I've got to get back to Earth, Lynn.
I'm here for a few months. I've got experiments to run. Have a safe trip home.
Returning to Earth can be just as dangerous as leaving it. Friction from air slows down a spacecraft coming out of orbit.
The spacecraft experiences extreme temperatures as it streaks through Earth's atmosphere.
But the service and crew modules that brought us here are also our safe ride home.

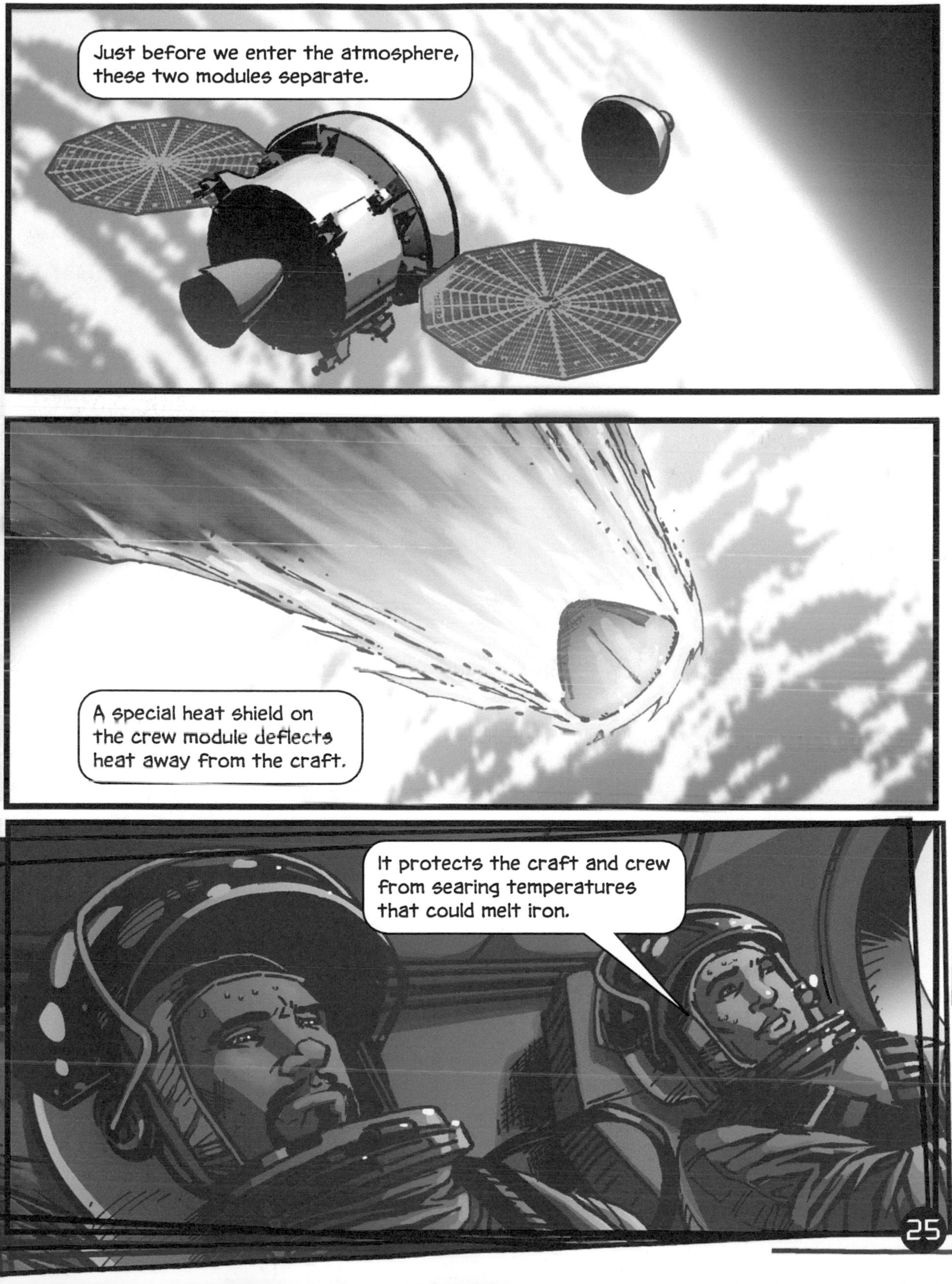
Just before we enter the atmosphere, these two modules separate.
A special heat shield on the crew module deflects heat away from the craft.
It protects the craft and crew from searing temperatures that could melt iron.

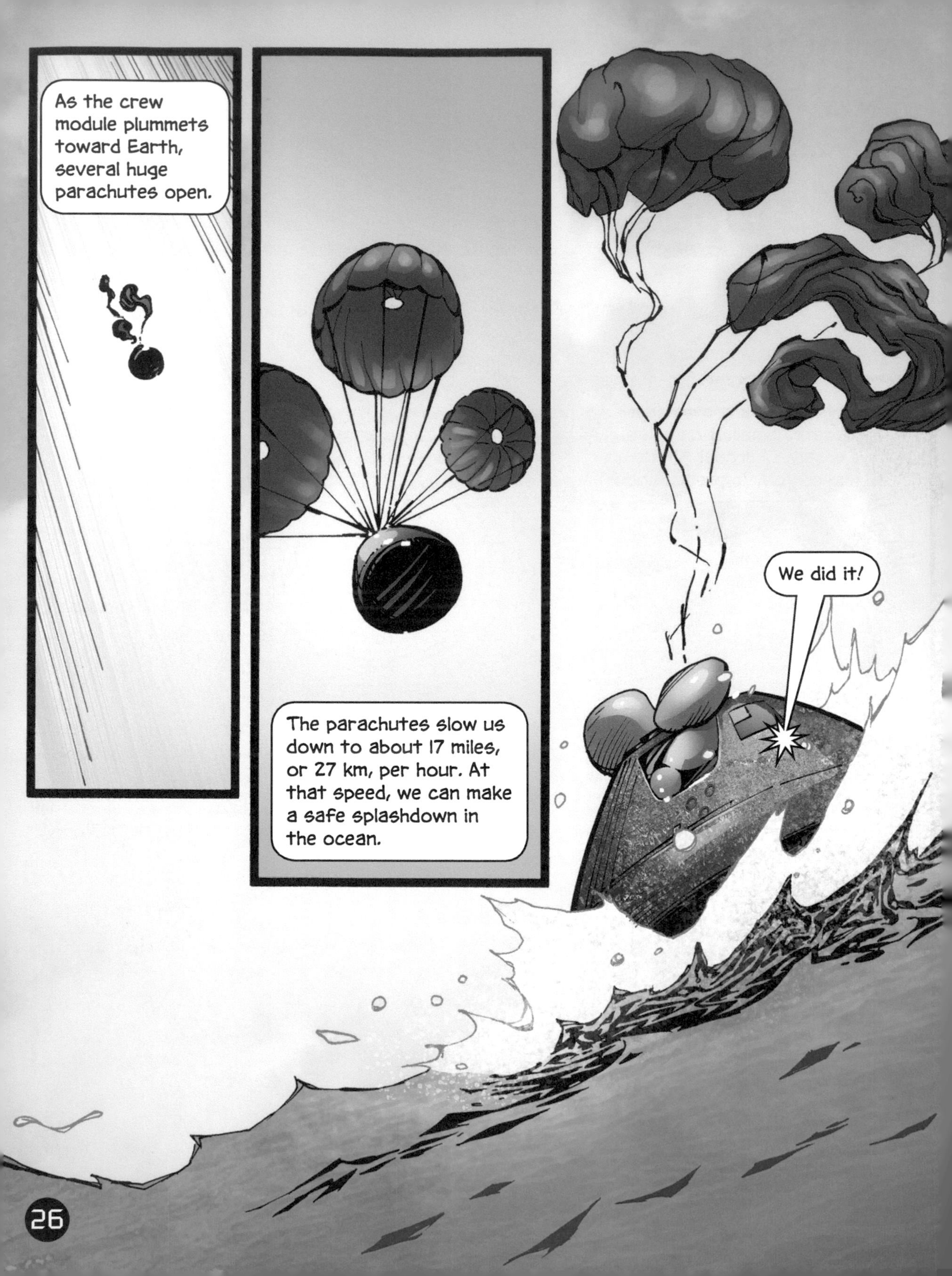
As the crew module plummets toward Earth, several huge parachutes open.
The parachutes slow us down to about 17 miles, or 27 km, per hour. At that speed, we can make a safe splashdown in the ocean.
We did it!

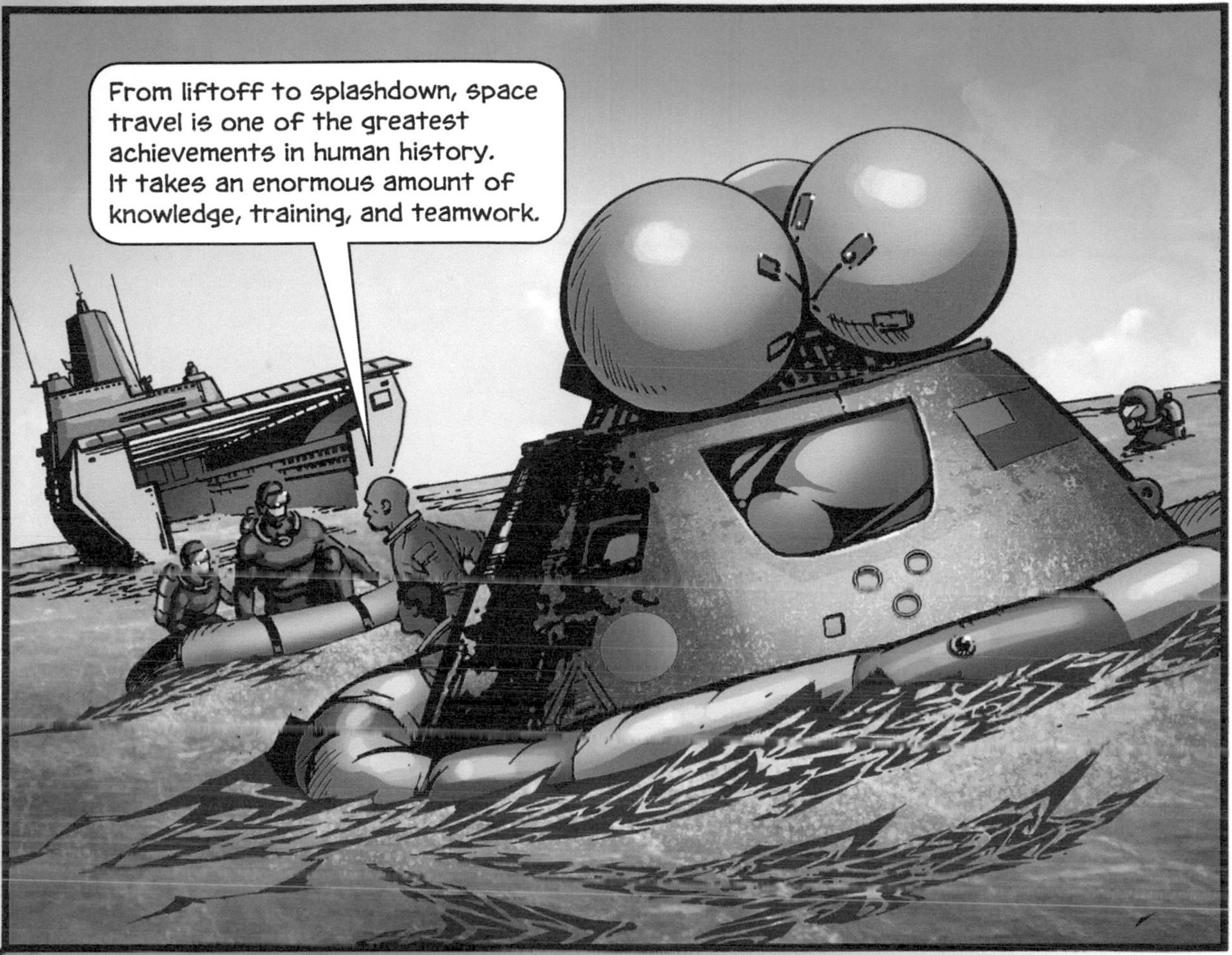
From liftoff to splashdown, space travel is one of the greatest achievements in human history. It takes an enormous amount of knowledge, training, and teamwork.

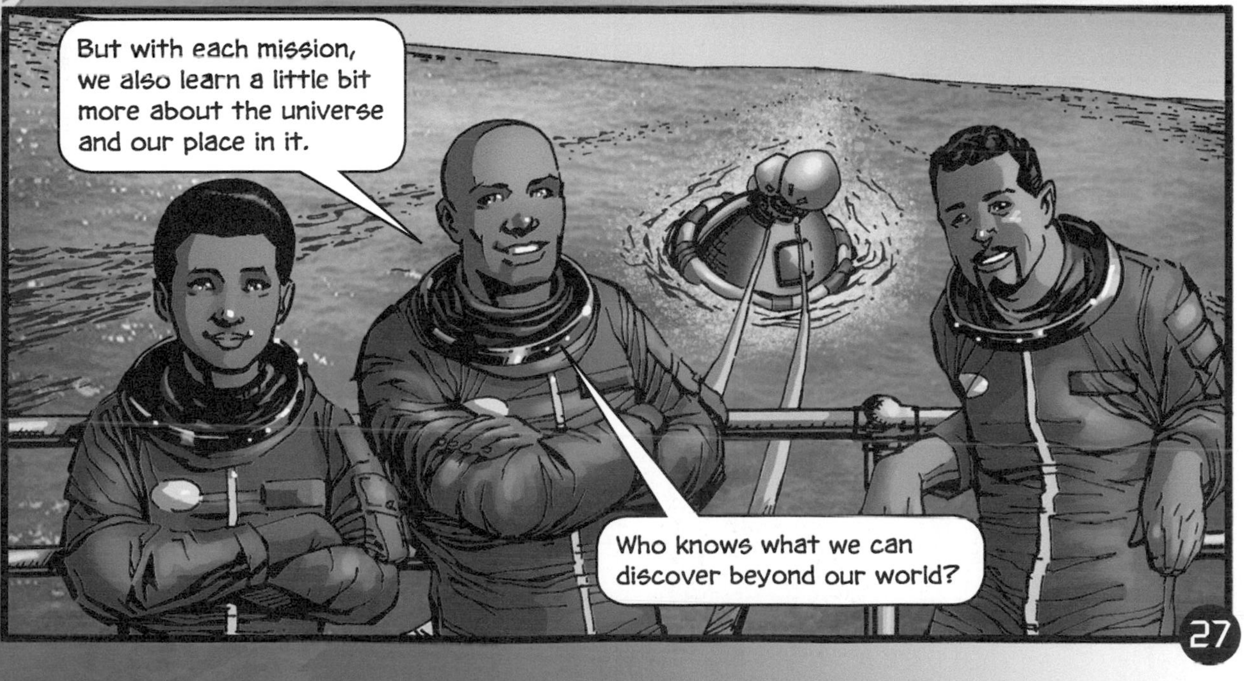
But with each mission, we also learn a little bit more about the universe and our place in it.
Who knows what we can discover beyond our world?

MORE ABOUT
SPACE TRAVEL

Rockets are different than jet engines. Jet engines require oxygen from the air to burn the fuel that they carry. Rocket engines need oxygen too. But they fly above the atmosphere where there's no air. Rockets have to carry their own oxidizer. This substance provides the oxygen needed to make fuel burn in the airlessness of space.

Space is so huge that astronomers measure distances in light-years. One light-year is the distance that light travels in one year. But just how far can light go in that time? In one year, it travels 6 trillion miles (10 trillion km). For light to reach the closest star to the sun, Proxima Centauri, it travels for four years. In comparison, our fastest spacecraft would take 19,000 years to travel the same distance.

Between 1969 and 1972, the United States sent 12 astronauts to the moon's surface in separate missions. Neil Armstrong and Buzz Aldrin became the first people to step on the moon in July 1969. About 18 months later astronaut Alan Shepard hit a few golf balls while he was there. In December 1972 astronauts Eugene Cernan and Harrison Schmitt became the last men to walk on the moon. No one has been there since.

It takes many months of study and training to become an astronaut. Astronauts have to learn their craft's systems, flight safety and operations, and land and water survival techniques. They also have to learn how to perform their duties in space. Floating in water is similar to floating in space. Astronauts train in their space suits in huge tanks of water.

CRITICAL THINKING USING THE COMMON CORE

1. What law of motion does a rocket use to overcome the pull of Earth's gravity? Where else in your daily life do you see this law of motion at work? (Key Ideas and Details)

2. How is living in a space station different from living in a house or an apartment? What types of things do astronauts need to survive that we take for granted on Earth? (Key Ideas and Details)

3. What are the differences between the service module and the crew module of a spacecraft? How do each of these parts help astronauts travel in space? (Integration of Knowledge and Details)

MORE ABOUT

SUPER SCIENTIST

Real name: Maxwell J. Axiom
Hometown: Seattle, Washington
Height: 6' 1"   Weight: 192 lbs
Eyes: Brown   Hair: None

Super capabilities: Super intelligence; able to shrink to the size of an atom; sunglasses give x-ray vision; lab coat allows for travel through time and space.

Origin: Since birth, Max Axiom seemed destined for greatness. His mother, a marine biologist, taught her son about the mysteries of the sea. His father, a nuclear physicist and volunteer park ranger, schooled Max on the wonders of earth and sky.

One day on a wilderness hike, a megacharged lightning bolt struck Max with blinding fury. When he awoke, Max discovered a newfound energy and set out to learn as much about science as possible. He traveled the globe earning degrees in every aspect of the field. Upon his return, he was ready to share his knowledge and new identity with the world. He had become Max Axiom, Super Scientist.

GLOSSARY

artificial (ar-tuh-FI-shuhl)—made by people

atmosphere (AT-muhss-fihr)—the mixture of gases that surrounds Earth

dehydrated (dee-HY-dray-tuhd)—having the water removed

engineer (en-juh-NEER)—someone trained to design and build machines, vehicles, bridges, roads, or other structures

exhaust (ig-ZAWST)—the waste gases produced by an engine

filter (FIL-tuhr)—a device that cleans liquids or gases as they pass through it

garment (GAR-muhnt)—a piece of clothing

gravity (GRAV-uh-tee)—a force that pulls objects with mass together; gravity pulls objects down toward the center of Earth

module (MOJ-ool)—a separate section that can be linked to other parts

orbit (OR-bit)—to travel around an object in space; an orbit is also the path an object follows while circling an object in space

oxidizer (OK-si-dahy-zer)—a substance that allows rocket fuel to burn in space

radiation (ray-dee-AY-shuhn)—rays of energy given off by certain elements

satellite (SAT-uh-lite)—a spacecraft that circles Earth; satellites gather and send information

weightlessness (WATE-liss-ness)—a state in which a person feels free of the pull of Earth's gravity

READ MORE

Baker, David, and Heather Kissock. *Living in Space.* Exploring Space. New York: Weigl Publishers, 2009.

Enz, Tammy. *Zoom It: Invent New Machines that Move.* Invent It. Mankato, Minn.: Capstone Press, 2012.

Halls, Kelly Milner. *Astronaut.* Cool Science Careers. Ann Arbor, Mich.: Cherry Lake Pub., 2010.

Hense, Mary. *How Astronauts Use Math.* Math in the Real World. New York: Chelsea Clubhouse, 2010.

Sparrow, Giles. *Space Exploration.* Space Travel Guides. Mankato, Minn.: Smart Apple Media, 2012.

Tagliaferro, Linda. *Who Walks in Space?: Working in Space.* Wild Work. Chicago: Raintree, 2011.

INTERNET SITES

FactHound offers a safe, fun way to find Internet sites related to this book. All sites on FactHound have been researched by our staff.

Here's all you do:

Visit *www.facthound.com*

Type in this code: 9781476501246

Check out projects, games and lots more at
www.capstonekids.com

INDEX